Creating Scientists

This book shows you how to create living, breathing scientists by shifting your teaching from a content focus to a hands-on, practice focus, where students discover science by doing science. As required by the new Next Generation Science Standards (NGSS), this practical book provides a clear, research-verified framework for building lessons that teach science practice abilities, such as gathering and making sense of data, constructing explanations, designing experiments, and communicating information. *Creating Scientists* features reproducible, immediately deployable tools and handouts that you can use in the classroom to assess your students' learning within the domains for the NGSS or any standards framework that focuses on the integration of science practice with content. This book is an invaluable resource for educators seeking to build a "community of practice," where students discover ideas through well-taught, hands-on, authentic science experiences that foster an innate love for learning how the world works.

Christopher Moore is the Dr. George F. Haddix Community Chair in Physical Science and associate professor of physics education at the University of Nebraska Omaha.

Also Available from Routledge
Eye On Education
www.routledge.com/eyeoneducation

STEM by Design: Strategies and Activities for Grades 4–8
Anne Jolly

The STEM Coaching Handbook:
Working with Teachers to Improve Instruction
Terry Talley

DIY Project Based Learning for ELA and History
Heather Wolpert-Gawron

DIY Project Based Learning for Math and Science
Heather Wolpert-Gawron

Write, Think, Learn: Tapping the Power of Daily Student Writing
Across the Content Areas
Mary K. Tedrow

The Genius Hour Guidebook:
Fostering Passion, Wonder, and Inquiry in the Classroom
Denise Krebs and Gallit Zvi

Writing Science Right
Strategies for Teaching Scientific and Technical Writing
Sue Neuen and Elizabeth Tebeaux

Rigor in the Classroom: A Toolkit for Teachers
Barbara R. Blackburn

Rigor and Assessment in the Classroom
Barbara R. Blackburn

put into place by professional scientists and their views about the discipline; however, you may be surprised by how students view science and its practices. We will examine the typical student's view of what science is and compare that to the expert's view, exposing the wide gap between the two. This will be important when we start to look at how to teach practices in the next chapter. If we aren't careful, the laboratories and many classroom activities we use could actually *reinforce* the student's novice view of science, and lead to the propagation of poor practices.

As we continue this chapter, we'll look at what the Next Generation Science Standards (NGSS) expects students should be able to do with respect to science practices throughout their K–12 education. I'll define science practices more explicitly, as they are outlined in the National Research Council's excellent document *A Framework for K–12 Science Education* (which I'll refer to as simply the *Framework* throughout the rest of the book; National Research Council, 2012). We'll also examine how these science practices are integrated within the performance expectations in the NGSS.

How Do Students View the Practice of Science?

My own research and that of my colleagues over the past decade has shown that fundamentally, the major distinction between the novice student and the expert scientist is in the way they think about and view science and its practice (Moore, 2012). In particular, the psychology and education professor Deanna Kuhn suggests that the distinction is most clear through their "epistemological appreciation" of how new knowledge is formed (Kuhn, 2004). Epistemology is the study of the nature of knowledge and how we go about acquiring knowledge. This is very relevant to our discussion about science practice, because it turns out that how a student views the practice of science is fundamentally a function of their epistemological beliefs (Edmondson & Novak, 1993).

As one example, the novice student will often make subconscious justifications for the way they practice science based on their view that science knowledge is "propagated stuff." They use a specific equation to solve some problem because an expert told them that that is how it should be done. Or, they learn that the mitochondria is the "powerhouse of the cell" from their textbook or class lecture. Maybe they memorize the periodic table of the elements for recall on an exam in the future. All of this

1

What Is Science Practice?

"Science practices are 'habits of mind' of scientists and engineers, things that they do on a regular basis in their work."

—The Rutgers Physics and Astronomy Education
Research Group (Etkina et al., 2017)

If we want to teach students science practices, then we first have to define what we mean by the term. Fundamentally, science practices are simply those things that expert scientists do. If we can teach students to think and act like practicing scientists, then they will learn the community accepted practices for discovering new truths about the physical world around them. It seems simple enough, but it does present the question: What exactly does a scientist do? What does it mean to be a capable scientist? How does an expert practice science, and how does a novice student *think* it should be practiced? The focus of this chapter is on answering these questions.

First, we'll look at how students *think* science should be done, and then we'll look at how scientists actually do science. As an educated science teacher, you will probably not be surprised by the types of practices

Part I

Teaching and Assessing Science Practice

Kuhn, D. (2004). What is scientific thinking and how does it develop? In U. Goswami (Ed.), *Blackwell Handbook of Childhood Cognitive Development*. Malden, MA: Wiley-Blackwell.

NGSS Lead States. (2013a). APPENDIX A—Conceptual Shifts in the Next Generation Science Standards. In N. L. States (Ed.), *Next Generation Science Standards: For States, by States*. Washington, DC: The National Academies Press.

NGSS Lead States. (2013b). *Next Generation Science Standards: For States, by States*. Washington, DC: The National Academies Press.

U.S. Census Bureau. (2012). *American Community Survey.* Retrieved from https://www.census.gov/programs-surveys/acs/

U.S. Census Bureau. (2014). *Educational Attainment in the United States.* Retrieved from https://www.census.gov/data/tables/2014/demo/educational-attainment/cps-detailed-tables.html space to really show off the science practices they have learned in your class. We'll also discuss how to use the framework discussed in the book to build new lessons based on your content objectives, and how to go beyond the NGSS when necessary.

Let's Create Some Scientists Together

Scientists are not born, they must be created. Even those famous scientists we know and love started out just like the curious kids we surround ourselves with daily: fascinated by the world around them, but with no real systematic understanding of how to learn more. They had to work hard to learn how the scientists they looked up to practiced their craft, and how to use those practices to discover new knowledge. Some were terrible at school and became great scientists in spite of their hatred of formal schooling. Unfortunately, many potentially great scientists never became scientists at all because the old science education system failed them.

If we simply try to cram facts into the brains of curious kids, then we risk killing their wonder. They can start to view science and the world around them as a known collection of stuff and laws, to be learned by reading a book. That is both boring and an inaccurate picture of science. Let us teach students that science is a wonderful process that they can use to discover.

Let us create some scientists together.

Note

1 "Next Generation Science Standards" is a registered trademark of Achieve. Neither Achieve nor the lead states and partners that developed the Next Generation Science Standards were involved in the production of this product, and they do not endorse it.

References

Department for Professional Employees. (2016). *The STEM Workforce: An Occupational Overview*. Washington, DC: AFL-CIO.

Donovan, M. S., & Bransford, J. D. (2005). Introduction. In N. R. Council (Ed.), *How Students Learn: History, Mathematics, and Science in the Classroom*. Washington, DC: The National Academies Press.

together to build truth from evidence, and reflect on those truths and the processes they used in their acquisition. I will also discuss the importance of being very explicit in your activities about what the students are doing and why they are doing it, having the students reflect on their learning, and making science practices "count" when grading.

How do you know whether or not your students are getting any better at science practice? Unfortunately, there is no simple test we can deploy in the classroom to measure practice abilities. In Chapter 3, I will describe how you can assess your students' growth as science practitioners by providing a framework for developing an entire assessable NGSS-based curriculum in your domain. We will discuss how to define learning goals, build learning experiences, and what to look for in student work as markers for success. I'll also show you how to incorporate experiments into summative assessments. Have you ever thought about using a laboratory activity as a test? Have your students ever reported *having fun* during a test? Mine do all the time!

Chapters 4–6 go through research-verified examples of classroom lessons that are based on the NGSS and are built from the framework described in the preceding chapters. You will see how we designed and deployed the lessons, examples of actual student work, how that work was assessed, and practical tips on how you can use the lessons in your classroom. The example content in this book focuses on physical science throughout the grade levels. However, it is important to point out that the science practices are cross-cutting, and just as valuable for the biology teacher or earth science content. Remember, I mentioned that content is just the context in which the lessons are done. You'll learn useful tips no matter what subject you teach.

I also have sneaky hidden agendas as you go through Chapters 4–6 on top of the examples of practice-based lessons. In particular, I will discuss how to transform a "traditional" lesson into a practice-teaching machine (Chapter 4), teach abstract concepts with no easily observable examples (Chapter 5), and build a community of practice in your classroom (Chapter 6).

And finally, Chapter 7 describes how you can put all the pieces together in capstone authentic explorations, where students go through the entire scientific process to solve some interesting problem, from identifying phenomena, observing, finding patterns, developing models, testing models, and communicating their findings in classroom-based scientific conferences. This is when we take the training wheels off and allow students

- Sample formative and summative assessment rubrics—to monitor progress and inform future teaching moves
- Frameworks for creating new assessment rubrics
- Checklists for quality "authentic science experiences" in the classroom

Furthermore, the end-of-chapter reference sections will lead you to the relevant literature, theory, and research so that you can understand why the activities work and can therefore develop and justify your own instruction using the same principles. My own research in science thinking and practice has shown that an explicit approach to these topics is required, where students are consistently required to think about their own thinking. The exact same approach is required for teachers to learn these abilities and learn how to teach them. Hopefully, you will think deeply about the content in this book by putting the lessons into practice, evaluating their effectiveness, and reassessing your own goals for your students.

An Outline

The first three chapters of the book answer three basic questions:

1. What is science practice?
2. How do you teach science practice?
3. How do you assess science practice?

In Chapter 1, I will describe what is meant by the term *science practice*. Specifically, I will discuss how experts do science, the practices they employ, and the ways they think about science. I will also describe how the student views science, the wide gulf between the student and the expert, and how "traditional" teaching can actually reinforce novice views of science and bad practices. We will look at the practices specified in the NGSS, which will serve as our example set throughout the rest of the book.

In Chapter 2, I will describe the framework you can use to teach science practice. In particular, I will discuss classroom-based *cognitive apprenticeship* as a framework you can use to teach science practice to your students. You will learn how to create *authentic science experiences* in the classroom, where students engage in authentic science practice, work

- Using mathematics and computational thinking
- Constructing explanations and designing solutions
- Engaging in argument from evidence
- Obtaining, evaluating, and communicating information

Every bit of that list is built into the NGSS. How do you teach a student to plan and carry out his or her own investigation? More importantly, how would you possibly assess something like that? Hopefully, once you've finished this book, you will have the tools necessary to answer those questions. Furthermore, you should have the tools necessary to build an authentic scientific community in your classroom, achieving what cognitive scientists call "a community of practice."

This book has the following learning outcomes for you the reader: After reading this book, you will be able to

1. Use a research-verified framework of generative principles to create your own lessons that improve the science practice abilities of your students
2. Assess your students' learning within these domains for the NGSS or any standards framework with focus on the integration of science practice with content
3. Link your approach to teaching to well-established research in science education

You will be able to track your personal growth and progress relative to these outcomes through the formative assessment methods described in the book. For those of you that are in-service teachers, the incorporation of immediately deployable, and research-verified classroom activities will allow you to begin implementation with known, effective materials. As you begin to use the framework to create new lessons, the growth in your teaching abilities will be trackable through assessment of your students' learning.

The book itself takes a *model-mentor-monitor* approach that mirrors the process of "cognitive apprenticeship" I am promoting throughout the book. Special features of this book include the following:

- Sample classroom activities—concrete models of how to do the work
- Frameworks for creating new activities—how to use the generative principles in the models for new situations

with the same set of practices that we are being asked to teach and assess. Ideally, this provides the student with a unified and coherent picture of what science is and how it is done so that it is consistent as they move up the grade levels, even though the sophistication may increase.

Finally, you are expected to teach toward a deeper understanding and application of content. What does "deeper understanding" really mean? It means that we want students to really learn content through the application of science practices in an authentic manner. We want students to discover content authentically, so that they understand not only the content, but also how science practice allows us to know that the content is true. This is exactly why the NGSS focuses on practices, and exactly why I am writing this book.

Unfortunately, what this all really means for you the practicing teacher is possibly a very dramatic rethinking of what you are doing in your classroom and the assessments you are using to evaluate your students' learning. I will not sugar coat it: The NGSS means more work for you. I hope the following chapters will help to lessen that burden.

What Will You Learn From This Book?

In the following chapters, I will provide

1. An approachable introduction to the relevant research on what science practice is, how it can be taught, and how it can be assessed, (something traditional science pedagogy does not achieve)
2. Specific, immediately deployable classroom activities
3. A framework you can use to create new lessons for your specific content needs—all in the context of next generation standards worldwide, like the Core Standards and NGSS in the United States

The framework and activities described in the book are research verified and will provide you the classroom tools necessary to help your students obtain the following abilities:

- Asking questions and defining problems
- Developing and using models
- Planning and carrying out investigations
- Analyzing and interpreting data

What Does This Mean for You, the Busy Teacher?

It is probably an understatement to say that teachers are not big fans of implementing big changes in standards. The tough, in-the-trenches work falls squarely on your shoulders. The NGSS does represent a fundamentally new paradigm for teaching and assessing science, but it is one that is desperately needed. What does this new paradigm mean for you, besides more work?

The NGSS writing teams identified several "conceptual shifts" that you, the science educator will need to make to effectively use the new standards (NGSS Lead States, 2013a). For the purposes of this book, I want to highlight three of these conceptual shifts. The shifts are as follows:

1. K–12 science education should reflect the real-world interconnections in science.
2. Science concepts build coherently across K–12.
3. The NGSS focus on deeper understanding and application of content.

Science education should reflect the real-world interconnections in science. Those interconnections many times manifest in content, but where the sciences are *really* connected are with respect to practices. Biology, chemistry, physics, and earth science are now expected to highlight these cross-cutting practices and make sure our students know that the types of abilities they are learning in biology class directly carry over to chemistry class. At the elementary level, this is easier in principle, because typically the same teacher is covering all of those disciplines. However, as the teaching of science breaks off into separate courses, it can be more complicated to coordinate across disciplines. The NGSS makes sure we all focus on the same cross-cutting practices from classroom to classroom.

Another conceptual shift you will need to make in your teaching is that science concepts build coherently across K–12. As you will see, the science practices you are expected to teach and assess are *the same across all age groups*. As a former high school physical science teacher, I know too well that it is easy to build walls around our little domains. We often fail to realize what students are even learning in middle school, much less elementary school. It was hard enough for me to get a handle on the state-based standards in my little area, not to even mention other age group's standards. With the NGSS, we are all playing on the same team, working two separate lessons. One on content, the next on graphs. Maybe the graphs lesson happens sometime later in the academic year, so long as it eventually happens.

However, within the practice of science, these dimensions are intimately linked. So-called neo-Piagetian studies of expert/novice practice demonstrate that cognitive abilities are not independent of content, experience, or environment (Kuhn, 2004). A learner best deploys practices within context, where content learning and practice are interrelated. Basically, if we want to immerse our students in authentic science, then we must not separate the practice of science from the content. Scientists do not think in terms of specific content *and then* specific practices.

Let us look at how the performance expectations in the NGSS handle the integration of content and practice. To preview, many of the expectations provided in the NGSS start similarly to the following:

Students who demonstrate understanding can

1. Construct an argument supported by empirical evidence to support . . . [content]
2. Develop a model based on evidence to illustrate . . . [content]
3. Analyze and interpret data on the . . . [content]
4. Construct, use, and present arguments to support the claim that . . . [content]
5. Conduct an investigation to provide evidence that . . . [content]

Each of these shorter segments is followed by some specific content, but the beginning is similar across *all* content for each grade level. From this, we can really start to see the tight integration of practice and content within the NGSS. There can be no separation of content and practice going forward, which means we have to re-think our teaching strategies.

Within the structure of the NGSS, students demonstrate understanding of a particular topic by showing they can practice science within that domain. In fact, there is not one instance of a performance expectation within the entire NGSS across K–12 where a student is simply expected to *"demonstrate understanding of . . .* [content]." What does it mean to demonstrate understanding? Is memorization understanding? No. All content is integrated with corresponding action statements of practice, because to understand science content, the student must understand how that content becomes scientific in the first place.

workshops and seminars, I always like to remind my audience that some of the students sitting in their classrooms will be our future politicians. Think about what you would rather have that student be able to do 10–20 years later: Draw a perfect diagram of the water cycle, or have the habits of mind to construct arguments supported by empirical evidence? We weirdos should hope that the "normals" all around us can at least understand and appreciate what scientists actually do.

The Next Generation Science Standards and the Coming Paradigm Shift in Science Teaching

For busy teachers like you and I, teaching and assessing science practice is about to be a very big deal, whether we want it to be or not. The Next Generation Science Standards (NGSS)[1] and other new state-based science standards are coming online, and these new standards require teachers to teach and assess science practice in the context of content (NGSS Lead States, 2013b).

Before the NGSS, most science standards at the individual state and district levels, along with standard science education practices, separated these dimensions. Specifically, science practice performance expectations would be separate from content expectations. Although not necessarily the intention, this separation had the practical effect of each dimension being taught and assessed individually. Let us look at the following two generalized performance expectations:

The student will be able to

1. Demonstrate an understanding of [content]
2. Graph the relationship between an independent and dependent variable

The first expectation is easily "assessed" using the ages-old standardized multiple-choice test, in many cases requiring little more than rote memorization to master. Whether actual understanding is achieved and whether the assessment is accurately measuring understanding is debatable. The second expectation can be assessed by examination of a student's work completing the task. The context of the task is irrelevant to the expectation. To the teacher, these two performance expectations signify

What isn't strange is having a curiosity about the world. Any teacher of young children knows that almost *all* children are incredibly curious about the world around them. They are immediately drawn to science because of its power to explain the mysteries all around them. As a species, we're hardwired to want to make sense of our world. However, only a tiny fraction of these children will ever grow up to become scientists.

We may be born with a driving curiosity, but the practical tools needed to *do* science must be learned, and therefore taught. Unfortunately, we can also destroy our young students' love of science through a constant focus on content, content, content—a focus that has been subconsciously beaten into our brains by our school teachers and college science professors, and possibly reinforced by state standards that look more like checklists of content than guides to learning about how science works.

As science teachers, it is our job to teach science. What that means, though, deserves a deeper discussion. That is what this book is all about. Is it our job to just teach "science facts"? Can we create great biologists by forcing students to memorize the parts of the cell? If the physical science student learns enough equations, are they then prepared to solve new challenges and make new discoveries? Is a chemist born the moment he or she has learned all of the elements on the periodic table? Are flash cards and memory tasks really a good way to excite the next generation about the practice of science?

In this book, I am going to argue for a philosophy of teaching science where the content is intimately integrated with practice. You will learn how to teach science practice in the context of content, instead of content first, and maybe a laboratory exercise here and there that reinforces the content. We know young students love to actively engage in the process of science, and that actual scientists don't just read about stuff in books. To create new scientists, we're going to need to build a classroom where students learn the practices of science, and then use those practices to discover content. We're going to need to build a "community of practice," where students discover ideas through well-taught, hands-on, authentic science experiences that foster their innate love for learning how the world works.

For most of our students, high school represents the termination of their formal science education. By that point, we would love for all of our students to have gained some abilities that will serve them well as informed citizens, such as analyzing and interpreting data, arguing from evidence, defining problems, and recognizing the tentative nature of knowledge. In at creating scientists, as evidenced by this room full of them. Why change something that has been working for hundreds of years?

Nearly every time I give a lecture or conduct a workshop with a group of professional scientists, I am asked a version of this question, no matter where in the world I happen to be. When I conduct workshops with science teachers, I am also usually asked a version of this question. After fielding this specific question numerous times in my career, I have developed a pretty good answer: *I'm weird, and so are you.*

I'm weird, and chances are if you're reading this book, you're pretty weird yourself. When I finished high school, I decided to go to college. Only about 34% of the U.S. population has a college degree, so that makes me a little weird (U.S. Census Bureau, 2014). I also decided to study science. Even weirder. In particular, I chose a major in physics, which is a choice made by less than 1% of all college students. Less than 1% of 34% of the population. Very strange.

After finishing my degree, I started teaching physical science at the secondary level. It's really weird to want to teach these subjects, so the United States has a serious supply/demand imbalance, with great jobs in school districts across the country going unfilled. The situation is the same around the globe. That means that science teachers are a truly strange, weird bunch.

As a scientist, I'm weird. As a science educator, I'm actually even weirder. Scientists and engineers make up only about 6% of the workforce in the United States (Department for Professional Employees, 2016). Science teachers represent less than 1% of the workforce. All of the scientists and science educators around the world took a similar strange and weird path to my own. They constantly chose to be weird in the face of overwhelming odds. Less than 40% of college students that choose science or engineering majors end up with a science or engineering degree. About three-quarters of those that do get their degree end up working in a field other than science or engineering (U.S. Census Bureau, 2012).

Here's my point: We are outliers. We are the "success" stories. We are strange, and those students that sit in front of us each and every morning are normal. I want you to keep that in mind as you read this book. There is something about you that is different from your students. You think different than they do. You are the weird one, not them. You became a science educator despite pedagogies and foci proven to fail your normal friends. You're strange.

Introduction: How Do You Create Scientists?

"You are the owners and operators of your own brain, but it came without an instruction book. We need to learn how we learn."
—M. Suzanne Donovan and John D. Bransford (2005, p. 10)

Recently, I was presenting a talk about reformations in science education to a group of distinguished scientists from all over the world. This group was composed of brilliant scientists at the top of their fields and working at some of the most prestigious universities. In my presentation, I talked about coming changes to science education standards in the United States, and how new pedagogy and assessments would be needed. I showed slide after slide of data that demonstrated traditional models for science instruction fail. And most important to me, I talked about how an almost obsessive focus on teaching more and more content has resulted in the de-emphasis of the types of activities that really excite children: the hands-on practice of science.

After my presentation, a physicist from a well-known flagship university in the United States stood up to ask me a question, which I paraphrase as follows:

> Everyone in this room went through programs based on the traditional sage-on-the-stage, lecture-based model. It obviously worked

science. These workshops were the brainchild of Laura Williamson, the recently retired director of curriculum and instruction at Prince Edward County Public Schools. This direct work with some amazing teachers launched my interest in formal science education research over a decade ago, leading right through to today and to this book.

I am not sure whether I should thank my family or apologize. My wife Kelly and children Balin and Rory had to put up with my absence for extended periods of time while I hid away in our little home office. As I sit here writing this acknowledgment late into the evening, I'm realizing that it's Father's Day and I've barely seen any of them. Yay deadlines! They never stopped loving me for some reason, and for that I am grateful. My children's love of science but absolute hatred of formal schooling was certainly a motivator to eventually get this book into the hands of practicing educators. Thankfully, the acknowledgments section is always the last to be written, so I'll soon be seeing a lot more of them.

Finally, I want to acknowledge you for picking up this book and reading it. This book was written for science teachers, so there's a good chance you are one. I know all too well the struggle attached to that job. I've worked physical 10-hour shifts in heavy construction, and I've taught high school science. Teaching was harder. I know the feeling of coming home physically drained after digging trenches all day, and I know the feeling of coming home both physically and mentally drained after teaching physics all day to moody teenagers. Take away that amazing feeling you get from literally changing young lives for the better, and there is no way I would choose teaching. You could have chosen to do something easier, too, but you chose instead to devote your life to helping me as a parent make my kids awesome. Thank you. As a token of my appreciation, please accept this muddled mess of a book that I hope makes your job maybe just a tad bit easier.

Unfortunately for Josip, he managed to set into motion a chain of events that indirectly led to this book and to me placing on the back-burner some joint projects we had been working on. Thank you, Josip. Now that this thing is done, we'll be back at it soon.

You should probably know before you get too far into the book that I'm really a big phony. There are way smarter people out there that know way more about this stuff than I do. They are too numerous to list them all here by name, but if you go through the reference section at the end of each chapter, you'll find them. I read their books and papers and did my best to condense it and make sense of it all, hopefully to save you some time. I will mention Eugenia Etkina, Dewey Dykstra, Ramon Lopez, Lillian McDermott, and Paula Heron by name, though. I met Eugenia and Dewey in Puebla, too. During lunch and over the sound of some bad mariachi music that I'm sure is reserved only for gringo tourists, Eugenia introduced me to cognitive apprenticeship. Dewey is a radical proponent of radical constructivism. We talked about that and teaching physics to Buddhist monks, among other things. Ramon and I enjoyed a steak in Cordoba, Argentina. No one else at the conference wanted to join us. Steak in Argentina. Really? No one else? Ramon was co-chair of the NGSS writing team, so he definitely had a few words of wisdom for me. Lillian and Paula are giants in the field of physics education research and preparing future physical science teachers. The curriculum they developed for preservice teachers serves as the foundation of my own work. Because of conversations I had with each of them, I was set on a path that involved a lot of books. Most of those books are in the references, and the authors of those books did all of the real work for which I will try to claim all the glory. However, if something in this book sounds stupid or is just plain wrong, it's almost certainly my fault and not theirs. They did the heavy lifting. I'm just the messenger doing my best to not turn this whole thing into a terrible game of telephone.

Over the years, the National Science Foundation (NSF) has given me a ridiculous amount of your tax dollars so that I could do the research that I talk a little about in this book. The Division on Undergraduate Education at the NSF awarded me and my colleague Louis Rubbo a grant (NSF-DUE #1244801) to develop a physics course focused on science reasoning and practice for middle school education majors at Coastal Carolina University in Conway, SC. This only happened because I had previously received funding from Virginia Dominion Power to develop a series of workshops for elementary and middle school teachers on inquiry in

Acknowledgments

I was sitting with my wife at a bar in Berlin when I met Jeff Wilhelm. Jeff is Distinguished Professor of English Education at Boise State University, director of the Boise State Writing Project, and author or co-author of 36 books for educators. Jeff and I were at a social function for the Fulbright program in Europe, and we were completely surrounded by young English-language graduate teaching assistants and vibrating air molecules reproducing German technopop rather loudly in our ears. Between scavenging free beer tickets from teetotaling Fulbrighters, we talked about why we were both there. He was a Fulbright Scholar in Germany in English education, and I was in the Czech Republic working on a science education project.

It turns out that before arriving in Germany, Jeff had been working on a science literacy project in Idaho and had been looking for research-based NGSS materials for the project. He had come up short and got pretty excited when I told him I worked in that area. Several beers previous to this discussion, I had thought very little about publishing a book on the topic. Now that alcohol had stolen from me the good sense to know better, Jeff had convinced me such a book was needed and that I should write it. He also convinced my wife, who, I should point out, wasn't going to have to actually write the thing. After getting back to Prague, I stayed in contact with Jeff. Between his and my wife's incessant badgering, I managed to cobble together a book proposal based on the series of seminars I had developed for middle school physical science teachers in Prague. And here we are. So really, this whole mess and my year-long lack of a social life as I wrote it is basically Jeff's fault. Thanks, Jeff.

I might not have had the time and motivation to put together the seminar series that led to this book if I hadn't been awarded the Fulbright Scholar award. Therefore, I need to thank the Fulbright U.S. Scholar program, the Czech Fulbright Commission, and my hosts at Charles University in Prague. Specifically, I thank Hana Ripková, Leoš Dvořák, Zdeněk Drozd, and Dana Mandíková. I had met Zdeněk and Dana in Puebla, Mexico, of all places. We were all conducting workshops for Latin American physics teachers at the invitation of my friend and collaborator Josip Slisko.

About the Author

Christopher Moore is the Dr. George F. Haddix Community Chair in Physical Science and associate professor of physics education at the University of Nebraska Omaha. Holding a M.S. in applied physics and a Ph.D. in chemistry from Virginia Commonwealth University, Dr. Moore has worked as a physical science teacher at several secondary schools in Virginia, as a professional materials scientist, and as a scholar of and consultant on science education. His education research focuses on the development of scientific reasoning and expert-like science practice abilities, with emphasis on practices that cross disciplines. This work has resulted in the publication of several dozen articles, invited speaker roles all over the world, and multiple awards including a Fulbright Scholar award. He has developed pre- and in-service teacher-training workshops on science practices in the Czech Republic, Mexico, and for school districts across the United States.

Printable versions of the tools in the book are available at Dr. Moore's website, www.creatingscientists.com.

Contents

About the Author viii
Acknowledgments ix

Introduction: How Do You Create Scientists? 1

PART I: TEACHING AND ASSESSING SCIENCE PRACTICE 13

1 What Is Science Practice? 15

2 How Do You Teach Science Practice? 35

3 How Do You Assess Science Practice? 56

PART II: SCIENCE PRACTICE IN THE CLASSROOM 85

4 Conducting Investigations and Transforming
   Your Classroom 87

5 Interpreting Results and Teaching Abstract Concepts 117

6 Communicating Science and Building Communities
   of Practice 142

PART III: PUTTING IT ALL TOGETHER 165

7 Capstones to Learning and Going Beyond the NGSS 167

This book is dedicated to my children, Balin and Rory. Classroom science should never crush their curiosity.

First published 2018
by Routledge
711 Third Avenue, New York, NY 10017

and by Routledge
2 Park Square, Milton Park, Abingdon, Oxon, OX14 4RN

Routledge is an imprint of the Taylor & Francis Group, an informa business

© 2018 Taylor & Francis

The right of Christopher Moore to be identified as author of this work has been asserted by him in accordance with sections 77 and 78 of the Copyright, Designs and Patents Act 1988.

All rights reserved. No part of this book may be reprinted or reproduced or utilized in any form or by any electronic, mechanical, or other means, now known or hereafter invented, including photocopying and recording, or in any information storage or retrieval system, without permission in writing from the publishers.

Trademark notice: Product or corporate names may be trademarks or registered trademarks, and are used only for identification and explanation without intent to infringe.

Library of Congress Cataloging-in-Publication Data
A catalog record for this book has been requested

ISBN: 978-1-138-23797-1 (hbk)
ISBN: 978-1-138-23798-8 (pbk)
ISBN: 978-1-315-29859-7 (ebk)

Typeset in Palatino
by Apex CoVantage, LLC

Creating Scientists

Teaching and Assessing Science Practice for the NGSS

Christopher Moore

Routledge
Taylor & Francis Group

NEW YORK AND LONDON

is science knowledge, but it isn't sense-making, in that they may know the fact but not necessarily the *why* and *how*. Their view of knowledge acquisition in the sciences, their epistemology, is that "experts" provide "facts."

If a student gets stuck in this mental framing in the science class, and it seems that they often do, then that student starts seeing science as merely a collection of facts, and experiments as mere ancillaries to learning those facts (Tsai, 1998). Obviously, we want to move students away from this naïve view about science, experiments, and the nature of knowledge formation, because this just isn't how science is practiced. If we want to create scientists, then we need students to start viewing science as a process of discovery.

We can actually learn a lot about how students view science from prior research. For example, the *Views About Sciences Survey* (VASS) is a relatively short and simple pencil-and-paper assessment that probes student views about science along six dimensions (Hestenes & Halloun, 1996):

1. Structure
2. Methodology
3. Validity
4. Learnability
5. Reflective thinking
6. Personal relevance

Over the past few decades, this assessment has been deployed in numerous science classrooms across the United States. From the results, we can build a fairly good picture of how the novice student views science across these dimensions. These novice student views are summarized in Table 1.1 (Hestenes & Halloun, 1998).

For the purposes of this book, let's focus on the first three dimensions of student views: structure, methodology, and validity. These three dimensions make up the foundational views used by students to construct an understanding of the practice of science. Specifically, results from the VASS suggest that students typically view the structure of science as being a collection of facts, the practice of science as situationally dependent, and the validity of science as being absolute, with no room for growth. Also note that students have an interesting view about how science is learned: *by memorizing facts*.

TABLE 1.1 TAXONOMY OF STUDENT VIEWS ABOUT SCIENCE.

Dimension	How Students View Science
Structure	Science is a loose collection of directly perceived facts.
Methodology	The methods of science are specific to the discipline.
Validity	Scientific knowledge is exact, absolute, and final.
Learnability	Science is learnable by a few talented people.
Reflective thinking	For meaningful understanding of science, one needs to memorize facts.
Personal relevance	Science is of exclusive concern to scientists.

Source : Adapted from (Hestenes & Halloun, 1998)

In contrast, Table 1.2 shows the stark difference between the novice student and the expert scientist in their views across these three dimensions (Hestenes & Halloun, 1998). The expert scientist recognizes the tentative nature of science that is an ever-expanding body of knowledge with cross-cutting methodologies. The scientist believes the learning of science happens through the practice of science.

What's really scary is that studies have shown that as students go through school, their views about science *actually get worse*! Our teaching could be pushing students *away* from expert-like views about science (Adams et al., 2006; Shan, 2013). How is this so? Let's think about a possible example where we readily give away the answers in the classroom. A student may ask: "Why is the air above the toaster wiggly?" As science teachers, we love getting questions like this from students, because they demonstrate genuine curiosity within those brains. But maybe we are a little too quick to launch into a lecture on air density and refraction. Once students know the answer, they have a fact. Imagine observing a magic act where the trick is revealed. You may nod your head and feel some satisfaction for learning a fact, but you are certainly no closer to becoming a magician. There is an art to the practice of magic that goes beyond knowing tricks.

What are we doing when we spend a majority of our time focusing on the teaching of facts in the science classroom? We are reinforcing this novice-like conception about science that it is a collection of facts to be learned, when science is really a process that leads to new knowledge. Just like you might walk away from our magic show assuming magic is a collection of tricks to be learned, and nothing more.

TABLE 1.2 TAXONOMY OF EXPERT-LIKE VIEWS ABOUT SCIENCE.

Dimension	How Scientists View Science
Structure	Science is a coherent body of knowledge about patterns in nature.
Methodology	The methods of science are cross-cutting.
Validity	Scientific knowledge is tentative and refutable.

Source: Adapted from (Hestenes & Halloun, 1998)

But what about the laboratory component of the science class? The middle school student might melt ice in a cup and measure the change in temperature as a function of the mass of the ice to demonstrate the already taught "law" that heat transfer is proportional to the mass. The high school student might use these same data to determine the heat capacity of the material. The student may drop items of varying weight from the bleachers to determine that they truly do fall at the same rate. These are examples where the answer is already known. Typically, the experiment is given to the student, too!

There is no real discovery for the student dropping items from the bleachers. It sure is fun, but the student is merely demonstrating a "fact" that he or she probably already "learned" in class. The hypothesis was set for them from the beginning, and the task itself dictated. The activity may do a great job of reinforcing the learning of content knowledge, but we can start to see how and why a young student might begin to view all science as stuff to be learned, instead of a process to be practiced, and how what we perceive to be quality, hands-on instruction is really reinforcing that naïve view.

As we'll learn in later chapters, a hands-on approach to science is an excellent way to get students engaged in learning. It's fun, which makes learning easier. However, if students view science as facts to learn, and you assess students on their ability to recall facts, then they will rightly conclude that all of that fun hands-on stuff is ancillary as opposed to fundamental. They'll miss the point of science.

So how do we move forward? How do we get students to start viewing science like scientists so that they can start practicing like them? The *Framework* mentioned above proposes a new approach to K–12 science education that advocates the tight integration of content with practice, so that student views can be moved more toward expert-like views. In particular, we can get students to learn content through discovery via expert-like practices, accomplishing the learning of both.

The following is a quote about the integration of content and practice from the *Framework*:

> [L]earning about science and engineering involves integration of the knowledge of scientific explanations (i.e., content knowledge) and the practices needed to engage in scientific inquiry and engineering design. Thus the framework seeks to illustrate how knowledge and practice must be intertwined in designing learning experiences in K–12 science education.
> (National Research Council, 2012, p. 11)

If we're going to get students to stop thinking of science as "stuff" to know, then we have to start teaching science as being more than collections of "stuff" discovered by long-dead scientists. Scientists see science as a process, so we need to have students learn science as a process. That means, you will need to start teaching science content through the practice of science, and assessing students' science practice abilities. By rethinking science teaching in these ways, you can start to guide students to better understanding of the nature of science as seen by the scientist.

How Do Experts Practice Science?

Now that we know how the student views science when they first walk through our doors, let's take a closer look at how experts actually do science. Table 1.2 tells us about how scientists view science, but how does this translate to what expert-like science practices look like?

The typical science textbook will usually start with a description of the "scientific method," generally with an illustration similar to that shown in Figure 1.1. The scientist comes up with a research question, generates tentative theories, deduces specific predictions to test those theories through experimentation, carries out the experiment, makes a judgment based on the result, and then repeats if necessary. This is what we might call the "traditional" view of what constitutes science practice.

The science education theorist Anton Lawson (2005) has proposed that scientific reasoning and its practice fundamentally has this more traditional structure, which he describes as being "hypothetico-deductive" in nature.

Figure 1.1 Schematic representation of the traditional "scientific method."

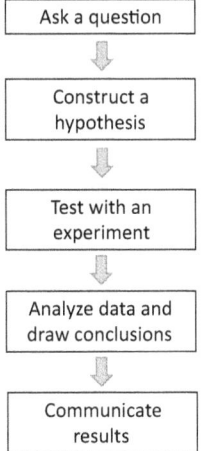

This means we make hypotheses and deduce the consequences. This aspect of science is primarily deductive. There are laws from which we deduce results. If the results are shown in reality, then the law is valid, otherwise the law must be revised.

There is no doubt that deductive process is at the heart of much of science practice; however, many practicing scientists, science philosophers, and education theorists and practitioners have concluded that this traditional view of science practice is just too simplistic a model of science alone to describe how science is done. Real, authentic science is much messier.

In particular, how do scientists come up with hypotheses in the first place? That is the key part missing from our simple scientific method schematic and should be an essential part of our teaching if we want to train future scientists. Science historian and philosopher Douglas Allchin (2003) argues that throughout the modern history of science, much of scientific discovery can be described as inductive in nature. What this means is that often scientists have *absolutely no clue* why or how certain phenomena occur, such that hazarding a guess, or hypothesis, would be of little value. Instead, scientists developed useful tools for identifying regularities, patterns, and associations. Instead of blindly identifying a hypothesis to test, observations can be made where patterns in the resulting data are used to devise a hypothesis.

The practice of science requires both deductive and inductive reasoning abilities, and the types of specific practices required to successfully use both to make new discoveries. In general, scientists make observations, identify evidence, generate and test hypotheses, and draw conclusions. We want our students to do all of that, too. Some of this is embedded in the "scientific method" shown in Figure 1.1. However, a lot of really important stuff is missing: pattern recognition; communication with the scientific community; how to use a model; structuring an argument. How do they come up with those neat experiments? How do they even know what questions to ask?

Why worry about being so clear about what the scientist does? Is it really that important in the elementary or middle school classroom? Let's imagine you follow a traditional deductive-only approach to teaching science, where you deploy worksheet labs having pre-existing hypotheses and a checklist procedure. The result will be a classroom full of students maintaining an unsophisticated understanding of science practice. Keep in mind, the student already views science as a collection of facts handed down by "others." If all we focus on is testing pre-existing hypotheses, which is the foundation of the "traditional" science laboratory, then we are basically telling students that their naïve view of science is correct. It's also dreadfully boring!

We want to expose students to the joy of true discovery. How can we learn more about this weird phenomenon? What does it depend on? Why does it behave like this when I do this other thing? We want to expose students to the "messy" side of science, where sometimes we do not know the answers. Sometimes we are wrong, and we have to re-evaluate our thinking. Sometimes we just have to play, twiddling a knob to see how it affects something else and trying to find some pattern.

Science Practices in the NGSS

What specific practices can we identify that will be relevant for the K–12 classroom? More importantly for you, the busy teacher, is determining the following: What are the science practices we are expected to teach and assess for the NGSS and how do they fit within our understanding of how real scientists practice their profession?

The *Framework* identifies eight essential practices of science and engineering that all students should learn, and the NGSS follows the

Framework's lead (National Research Council, 2012; NGSS Lead States, 2013b). Table 1.3 shows these practices, which I have separated into three dimensions: (1) investigation, (2) interpretation, and (3) communication. These are the three dimensions on which I base Chapters 4 through 6.

This is not an exhaustive list of practices used by professional scientists, but it is also not realistic to believe that high school graduates should be completely prepared for careers as professional scientists. The eight practices listed are an entry point for an informed citizenry that understands not only basic scientific content, but also the methods by which scientific knowledge is obtained.

First, the scientist must be able to ask good questions and define problems. Once the scientist has defined a problem and/or question, he or she can then begin to design and carry out an investigation, whether it is observation and looking for patterns, or testing a hypothesis. The scientist then either develops a model from their observations of patterns or uses a model in his or her testing. In Chapter 4, we'll go into more detail about the different types of investigations scientists do, how pattern recognition can lead to the generation of hypotheses and models, and how the student can mimic these processes throughout K–12.

Scientists and children really like the investigations. That's the fun part. But the scientists' job is not done yet, since they still must interpret their results. This often requires computational and/or mathematical thinking. From the analysis, scientists can then start to develop an explanation for observed behavior that can be tested, or design some solution to the problem they defined earlier. The second dimension of interpretation is as critical an aspect of the process of science and serves as the perfect

TABLE 1.3 SCIENCE PRACTICES IDENTIFIED IN THE FRAMEWORK.

Dimension	Science Practice
Investigation	◆ Ask questions and define problems ◆ Develop and use models ◆ Plan and carry out investigations
Interpretation	◆ Analyze and interpret data ◆ Use mathematics and computational thinking ◆ Construct explanations and design solutions
Communication	◆ Engage in argument from evidence ◆ Obtain, evaluate, and communicate information

Source: National Research Council (2012)

point for students to begin reflecting on what it is exactly that they are doing and learning. In Chapter 5, we'll describe interpretation in more detail and look at how to lead students toward developing more formal thinking about science.

Finally, science is a community endeavor. From observations of scientists practicing their craft, French sociologist Bruno Latour recognized that science is socially constructed (Latour, 1987). That is to say, the actual practice of science is less a method that is objectively applied, and more a process that is socially negotiated. A student in a group might question: "Why do this in this way? Wouldn't this over here be better?" And the negotiation begins. Scientists must learn to work within the scientific community to take part in this negotiation, and we as teachers must expose students to this dimension of communication in science. Students must communicate their work to others in the community, and they must always base their arguments on evidence to be taken seriously as members of the group. In Chapter 6, we'll look in more detail at facilitating this negotiation by building in the classroom what cognitive scientists Lave and Wegner (1991) call "communities of practice."

The complex manner in which these science practices interact as we do science is represented schematically in Figure 1.2. You'll notice that in

Figure 1.2 A more accurate model of how the scientist practices science.

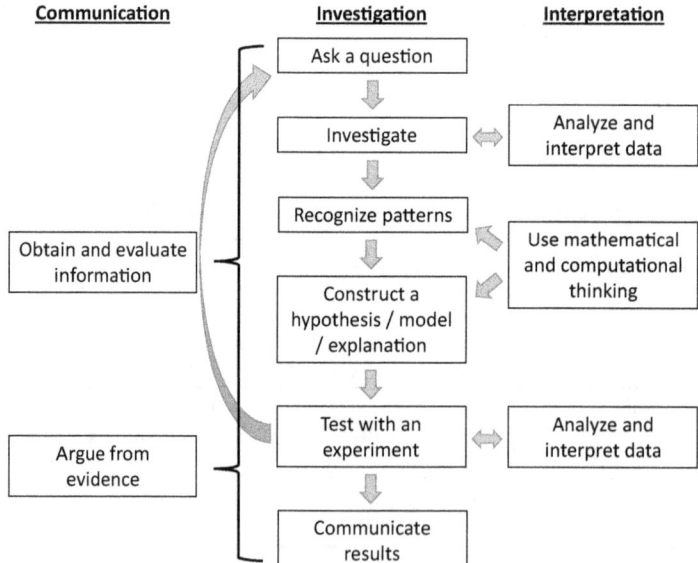

reality, the scientific method is more complex and fluid than we've been led to believe by textbooks and Figure 1.1. Furthermore, the practices themselves don't have easily identifiable "borders." An observation leading to a recognizable pattern necessarily becomes a lesson in argument from evidence and explanation construction. Working in a team to develop and use a model often requires abilities at analyzing data and using mathematics. In reality, the practices are intertwined. Keep Figure 1.2 in mind as you progress through the book.

All of this activity is actually quite a lot to handle, which is why the expert scientist has gone through extensive schooling, and typically many years of apprenticeship on the job and/or in graduate school working directly under a more seasoned expert. We do not expect our students to leave high school prepared to immediately tackle the great scientific questions of our age. However, we can begin by placing students on the right path, with those so inclined being ready for more schooling and apprenticeships.

Science Practices, Disciplinary Core Ideas, and Performance Expectations

Obviously, science content still needs to be taught. Teaching based on the *Framework* and the ideas expressed in this book may seem to focus on science practice, but bear in mind that science cannot be practiced except within the context of content. Within the NGSS, Disciplinary Core Ideas (DCIs) are the basic content we expect an educated citizenry to understand across the physical, chemical, and natural sciences (NGSS Lead States, 2013c). Within the NGSS, these ideas are consistent across the grade levels, where students are expected to build on and revise knowledge as they progress through the grade levels and acquire greater sophistication in science practice and cognitive ability. The NGSS also focus on a smaller set of content than many standards of the past. The intention here was that by focusing on a smaller set of core ideas, the teacher and student can develop a deeper understanding of concepts and their applications.

As I mentioned in the introduction, before the NGSS, most science standards at the individual state and district levels, along with standard science education practices, separated DCIs from practices. This separation

had the practical effect of each dimension being taught and assessed individually. Remember these two generalized performance expectations:
The student will be able to

1. Demonstrate an understanding of . . . [content]
2. Graph the relationship between an independent and dependent variable

However, within the framework of the NGSS, practices and content are intimately linked because cognitive abilities are not independent of content, experience, or environment. A learner best deploys practices within context, where content learning and practice are interrelated. As I discussed earlier, if we want to immerse our students in authentic science, then we must not separate the practice of science from the content. Scientists do not think in terms of specific content *and then* specific practices.

Let us look at how the performance expectations in the NGSS handle the integration of content and practice. Many of the expectations provided in the NGSS start similar to the following:
Students who demonstrate understanding can

1. Construct an argument supported by empirical evidence to support . . . [content]
2. Develop a model based on evidence to illustrate . . . [content]
3. Analyze and interpret data on the . . . [content]
4. Construct, use, and present arguments to support the claim that . . . [content]
5. Conduct an investigation to provide evidence that . . . [content]

Each of these shorter segments is followed by some specific content, but the beginning is similar across *all* content for each grade level. From this, we can really start to see the tight integration of practice and content within the NGSS. One of the eight science practices shown in Table 1.3 is used by the student in their discovery of whatever content we are interested in teaching that day. You can't make a peanut butter and jelly sandwich without *both* peanut butter and jelly. You can't teach science understanding without both practice and content.

Now, let's look at some examples of full performance expectations from the NGSS. Table 1.4 shows examples of performance expectations for each of the eight science practices detailed in Table 1.3 (NGSS Lead States, 2013c).

TABLE 1.4 EXAMPLES OF NGSS PERFORMANCE EXPECTATIONS FOR EACH SCIENCE PRACTICE.

Science Practice	Example NGSS Performance Expectation
Ask questions and define problems	**3-PS2–3.** Ask questions to determine cause and effect relationships of electric or magnetic interactions between two objects not in contact with each other. **MS-PS2–3.** Ask questions about data to determine the factors that affect the strength of electric and magnetic forces.
Develop and use models	**5-PS1–1.** Develop a model to describe that matter is made of particles too small to be seen. **MS-PS1–1.** Develop models to describe the atomic composition of simple molecules and extended structures. **HS-PS1–1.** Use the periodic table as a model to predict the relative properties of elements based on the patterns of electrons in the outermost energy level of atoms.
Plan and carry out investigations	**1-PS4–1.** Plan and conduct investigations to provide evidence that vibrating materials can make sound and that sound can make materials vibrate. **MS-LS1–1.** Conduct an investigation to provide evidence that living things are made of cells; either one cell or many different numbers and types of cells. **HS-PS2–5.** Plan and conduct an investigation to provide evidence that an electric current can produce a magnetic field and that a changing magnetic field can produce an electric current.
Analyze and interpret data	**K-ESS2–1.** Use and share observations of local weather conditions to describe patterns over time. **3-ESS2–1.** Represent data in tables and graphical displays to describe typical weather conditions expected during a particular season. **HS-ESS2–2.** Analyze geoscience data to make the claim that one change to Earth's surface can create feedbacks that cause changes to other Earth systems.
Use mathematics and computational thinking	**5-PS1–2.** Measure and graph quantities to provide evidence that regardless of the type of change that occurs when heating, cooling, or mixing substances, the total weight of matter is conserved. **HS-PS1–7.** Use mathematical representations to support the claim that atoms, and therefore mass, are conserved during a chemical reaction. **HS-ESS1–4.** Use mathematical or computational representations to predict the motion of orbiting objects in the solar system.
Construct explanations and design solutions	**1-PS4–2.** Make observations to construct an evidence-based account that objects in darkness can be seen only when illuminated. **MS-PS3–3.** Apply scientific principles to design, construct, and test a device that either minimizes or maximizes thermal energy transfer. **HS-PS1–5.** Apply scientific principles and evidence to provide an explanation about the effects of changing the temperature or concentration of the reacting particles on the rate at which a reaction occurs.

(Continued)

TABLE 1.4 (Continued)

Science Practice	Example NGSS Performance Expectation
Engage in argument from evidence	**2-PS1–4.** Construct an argument with evidence that some changes caused by heating or cooling can be reversed and some cannot. **MS-PS2–4.** Construct and present arguments using evidence to support the claim that gravitational interactions are attractive and depend on the masses of interacting objects. **HS-PS4–3.** Evaluate the claims, evidence, and reasoning behind the idea that electromagnetic radiation can be described either by a wave model or a particle model, and that for some situations one model is more useful than the other.
Obtain, evaluate, and communicate information	**2-ESS2–3.** Obtain information to identify where water is found on Earth and that it can be solid or liquid. **MS-PS1–3.** Gather and make sense of information to describe that synthetic materials come from natural resources and impact society. **HS-PS4–4.** Evaluate the validity and reliability of claims in published materials of the effects that different frequencies of electromagnetic radiation have when absorbed by matter.

Source: NGSS Lead States (2013c)

The performance expectation in the NGSS are labeled as follows:

GRADE LEVEL—DISCIPLINARY CORE IDEA—PERFORMANCE EXPECTATION

As an example, the first performance expectation listed in Table 1.4 is the following:

3-PS2–3. Ask questions to determine cause and effect relationships of electric or magnetic interactions between two objects not in contact with each other.

From the code that precedes each performance expectation, you can tell that this one is for the third grade, is within the domain of physical science (PS), and focuses on DCI PS2 (forces, motion, and types of interactions). It is the third performance expectation within this group. Similarly, a code of **MS-PS3–3** would correspond to the middle school age group, physical science, and DCI PS3 (Energy). You can find a listing of all of the DCIs and how they progress across age groups in Appendix E—Progressions

Within the Next Generation Science Standards listed in the references section of this chapter (NGSS Lead States, 2013a).

Science Practices Are Cross-Cutting

Now, let's look at how the performance expectations in the NGSS are connected across disciplines and across age groups. This is a critical component of the NGSS, and the focus of the first two conceptual shifts expected of educators using the *Framework* and the NGSS on which it is built: (1) that education should reflect the real-world interconnections across science disciplines, and (2) that practice builds coherently across the grade levels.

Science practices are cross-cutting, spanning the science disciplines, age groups, and even offering benefits outside of science. This is not a book about creating physicists or creating biologists. It is a book about creating scientists, and the NGSS is a set of standards aimed at doing the same. What are the types of practices that *all* scientists do? What abilities do good scientists have across the disciplines?

Instead of focusing on a student's skill at using a particular instrument for the chemistry class, you will be more interested in that student's ability to evaluate and minimize the uncertainty in the temperature measurement. You will want your students to develop the ability to create a mathematical model for a given electrical circuit, and then make a prediction based on that model. Because the NGSS demands it, you will want to assess whether your students can determine what variables are important to measure.

My own research and that of cognitive scientists has shown that science practices and reasoning abilities are often required for effective decision making and problem solving far outside the typical scientific context (Reif & Larkin, 1991; Moore & Slisko, 2017). This is why I think these types of abilities are *far* more important for an educated population than their ability to recall an equation, an element on the periodic table, or the names of structures found on diagrams of the cell. The writers of the NGSS agree, which is demonstrated by the significant focus on practices.

For example, below are two examples of performance expectations from the DCIs for both middle school life science and physical science, respectively:

> **MS-LS2–4.** *Construct an argument supported by empirical evidence* that changes to physical or biological components of an ecosystem affect populations.
>
> **MS-PS2–4.** *Construct and present arguments using evidence* to support the claim that gravitational interactions are attractive and depend on the masses of interacting objects.

What I want you to take away from this example is the focus that is being placed on the practice: engaging in argument from evidence. The types of data that a student might be looking at in the two different classes may be different, and the very specific analyzation techniques may differ, but the underlying practice is the same.

Let me show you another example, only this time across age groups. The following two performance expectations come from Kindergarten physical science and high school earth science, respectively:

> **K-PS3–1.** *Make observations to determine* the effect of sunlight on Earth's surface.
>
> **HS-ESS1–1.** *Develop a model based on evidence* to illustrate the life span of the sun and the role of nuclear fusion in the sun's core to release energy that eventually reaches Earth in the form of radiation.

In this case, the content is essentially the same (the Sun's radiation), with increasing sophistication with age. The practice dimension is also the same (investigation), again with increasing sophistication. In the early age groups, the NGSS has us start with teaching basic observation practices of the concrete world around us. As students develop, we increase the sophistication to the point where we expect them to be able to develop a hypothetical model based on these observations and other hypothetical models (in this case, fusion). The fundamental science practice is the same, though, for the Kindergartener and the high schooler.

There is a tendency within the science education publishing industry to split books up into various age groups, with one book for elementary school science teachers, one for middle school teachers, and one for high school teachers. However, if we want to discuss science practices in general, then this is a poor approach that reinforces the perception that we are all doing something different. One of the most important lessons that I hope to convey with this book is that the processes of science are the same. Science is science. In many cases, even the content is similar across age groups.

Science Practices vs. Science Skills

When thinking about science practices and the performance expectations, I want you to be careful. It's easy to confuse the concept of practices with that of skills. There is a subtle difference between what we consider "skills" and what we call "practices."

The National Resource Council in the *Framework* describes the difference between skills and practices as follows:

> We use the term "practices" instead of a term such as "skills" to emphasize that engaging in scientific investigation requires not only skill but also knowledge that is specific to each practice.
> (National Research Council, 2012, p. 30)

It goes deeper than that, though. Expert-like *practice* of science requires deep thinking and self-evaluation at all stages. As we have already discussed, the expert scientist is metacognitively aware, meaning they think about what they are doing, why they are doing it, and analyze their own thinking and practice as they go. In fact, good science practice demands this. Expert-like *skill* can be an automated process—something learned and repeated flawlessly without any further cognitive evaluation.

Let's look at a few examples to clarify the distinction. Teaching a student how to use a digital thermometer is a skill. The student can turn on the thermometer, attach an appropriate probe, position the thermometer at the point of measurement, adjust for the desired units, and read the resulting measurements. We can also teach a student how to calibrate the thermometer using a combination of boiling and ice water. Similarly, we can teach a student how to use a digital multi-meter to make measurements of current in a circuit. We can show them what the different symbols mean, which to select for which function, how to position the probes within the circuit, and how to read the measurement. Once learned and practiced a few times, the student will be able to pull out a thermometer or a meter and make measurements with no further thought.

Being able to use a thermometer and a digital multi-meter are skills. In many sub-disciplines of science and jobs in industry these skills are very necessary. They are also highly context-dependent. The zoologist will rarely if ever have need to measure current with a digital multi-meter. Being skilled at using a multi-meter will also not directly carry over to using zoological field instruments, like binoculars or GPS systems.

I do want to highlight that skills are important, and learning skills useful in one domain can make it easier to learn skills applicable to another domain. Furthermore, skills learning will be necessary for your students as they practice science within the classroom. After all, I can't imagine teaching a chemistry lab without students learning a plethora of necessary laboratory skills! The *Framework* and the NGSS, however, do not focus on skills, but they rather focus on practices. Obviously, you will be teaching your students domain-specific skills as they progress through their learning. However, not one of the NGSS performance expectations singles out any specific skill necessary for demonstrating understanding.

Summary

In this chapter, I have tried to answer the question, What is science practice? To this end, we have discussed how experts do science, the practices they employ, and the ways they think about science. I have briefly described the research into the ways students view science, the wide gulf between the student and the expert, and how "traditional" teaching can actually reinforce novice views of science and bad practices. And finally, we have looked at the practices specified in the NGSS, and we have discussed their cross-cutting nature, both across disciplines and across age groups.

The following is a brief summary of the key points:

- Science practices are those things scientists do.
- Students view science as a collection of facts with methods that are domain specific, which is a novice view that we can accidentally reinforce if we are not careful.
- Real science is tentative, ever expanding, and utilizes practices/methods that are cross-cutting across disciplines.
- Science practices can be separated into the following, interrelated dimensions:
    ◇ Investigation
    ◇ Interpretation
    ◇ Communication

- The NGSS integrates science content and practice in its performance expectations.
- Content and practice in the NGSS progresses across disciplines and age groups.
- Science practices are different from skills.

References

Adams, W. K., Perkins, K. K. Podolefsky, N. S., Dubson, M., Finkelstein, N. D., & Wieman, C. E. (2006). New instrument for measuring student beliefs about physics and learning physics: The Colorado learning attitudes about science survey. *Physical Review Special Topics—Physics Education Research*, 2(1), article number 010101.

Allchin, D. (2003). Lawson's Shoehorn, or should the philosophy of science be rated X? *Science and Education*, 12, 315–329.

Edmondson, K. M., & Novak, J. D. (1993). The interplay of scientific epistemological views, learning strategies, and attitudes of college students. *Journal of Research in Science Teaching*, 30, 547–559.

Etkina, E., Heuvelen, A. V., Brahmia, S., Brookes, D., Gentile, M., Karelina, A., . . . Zou, X. (2017). *Scientific Abilities: Introduction*. Retrieved from Rutgers Physics and Astronomy Education Research Group: https://sites.google.com/site/scientificabilities/

Hestenes, I., & Halloun, D. (1996). Views about sciences survey. *Annual Meeting of the National Association for Research in Science Teaching*. Saint Louis, Missouri: ERIC Document No. ED394840.

Hestenes, I., & Halloun, D. (1998). Interpreting VASS dimensions and profiles. *Science & Education*, 7(6), 553–577.

Kuhn, D. (2004). What is scientific thinking and how does it develop? In U. Goswami (Ed.), *Blackwell Handbook of Childhood Cognitive Development* (pp. 371–393). Malden, MA: Wiley-Blackwell.

Latour, B. (1987). *Science in Action: How to Follow Scientists and Engineers Through Society*. Milton Keynes, UK: Open University Press.

Lave, J., & Wenger, E. (1991). *Situated Learning: Legitimate Peripheral Participation*. New York: Cambridge University Press.

Lawson, A. E. (2005). What is the role of induction and deduction in reasoning and scientific inquiry? *Journal of Research in Science Teaching*, 42, 716–740.

Moore, J. C. (2012). Transitional to formal operational: Using authentic research experiences to get non-science students to think more like scientists. *European Journal of Physics Education*, 3(4), 1–12.

Moore, J. C., & Slisko, J. (2017). Dynamic visualizations of multi-body physics problems and scientic reasoning: A threshold to understanding. In T. Greczylo & E. Debowska (Eds.), *Key Competences in Physics Teaching and Learning*. New York, NY: Springer.

National Research Council. (2012). *A Framework for K–12 Science Education: Practices, Crosscutting Concepts, and Core Ideas*. Washington, DC: The National Academies Press.

NGSS Lead States. (2013a). APPENDIX E—Progressions Within the Next Generation Science Standards. In N. L. States (Ed.), *Next Generation Science Standards: For States, by States*. Washington, DC: The National Academies Press.

NGSS Lead States. (2013b). APPENDIX F—Science and Engineering Practices in the NGSS. In N. L. States (Ed.), *Next Generation Science Standards: For States, by States*. Washington, DC: The National Academies Press.

NGSS Lead States. (2013c). Standards by DCI. In N. L. States (Ed.), *The Next Generation Science Standards: For States, by States*. Washington, DC: The National Academies Press.

Reif, F., & Larkin, J. H. (1991). Cognition in scientific and everyday domains: Comparisons and learning implications. *Research in Science Teaching*, 28, 733.

Shan, K. J. (2013). Improving student learning and views of physics in a large enrollment introductory physics class. *Theses and Dissertations*, 205, 75–97.

Tsai, C.-C. (1998). An analysis of scientific epistemological beliefs and learning orientations of Taiwanese eighth graders. *Science Education*, 82(4), 473–489.

2

How Do You Teach Science Practice?

"Telling children how scientists do science does not necessarily lead to far-reaching changes in how children do science."

—Seymour Papert (1991)

Now that we have defined what is meant by "science practice," we can start looking at the research to see how we can effectively teach science practice. A shift in focus from traditional descriptive content knowledge toward an integration of knowledge and practice requires a similar shift in pedagogy. What pedagogies lead to demonstrated improvements in science practice abilities? The Next Generation Science Standards (NGSS) is purposefully agnostic on pedagogy, so we'll have to look to the research literature to see what has worked, and maybe more importantly, what has not worked. Then, we'll have to synthesize the literature into a workable framework for creating new lessons that meet the needs of your classroom.

In this chapter, I will discuss how science practice can be taught in context. Specifically, I will describe how to use the theoretical framework of *cognitive apprenticeship* to build an authentic community of practice within the classroom. You may have a good idea of where this chapter is headed if you have kept up with best practices in science teaching. After all, pedagogies based on inquiry learning, which has similarities to cognitive apprenticeship, have revolutionized the way we teach science over the past decade, and have proven to be significantly more effective over traditional lecture-based methods, at least with content learning and retention.

But is inquiry learning enough for new standards that explicitly call for teaching and assessing practice? What would successful inquiry methods look like in this new environment, if any different? The NGSS is fairly clear with its performance expectations for students, but what exactly are we supposed to do in the classroom to ensure students gain these science practice abilities? Is simply doing science in the classroom enough? The surprising answer that you'll find in this chapter is no, probably not!

Understand Why What You Do in the Classroom Works

This chapter will be fairly research heavy, with the "good" stuff to follow in Chapters 4–6. Often, teachers reach for very specific activities that they can use in their classroom right away, and maybe casually think about how those activities were developed. That's understandable. You're very busy, and the demands on teachers' time has only increased over the past few decades.

However, I really want you to resist the urge to immediately flip to the second part in the book. I think it is important for you to understand how these methods came to be. The most important reason is that without a firm grounding in the why, we can easily screw up the implementation. In particular, the inquiry-based methods that have become extremely popular in science education can fail miserably when poorly executed. As an example, later in this chapter I'll tell you how I've screwed up in my own classes. When you understand how the methods came about and why they work, then you will be significantly less likely to implement them incorrectly.

To help prepare you, I have provided a simple map in Table 2.1 that will serve as our guide for the first several sections. We will learn that much of the NGSS and the teaching methods that will best support them come from research in the following areas:

- Situated cognition
- Cognitive apprenticeship

TABLE 2.1 THEORIES OF LEARNING AND TEACHING ON WHICH THIS BOOK (AND THE NGSS) IS BASED.

Concept	Description
Situated cognition	*A theory of learning* where understanding requires abilities in practice as well as knowledge
Cognitive apprenticeship	*A theory of teaching* where the student is taught how to practice within the context of content

Situated cognition is a theory of learning. Cognitive apprenticeship is a theory of teaching. These two theories build on each other to produce a strong framework for the teaching and learning of science practice. At the end of the chapter, I will provide a checklist for building effective activities based on everything we learn from the research in these two areas. This checklist will serve as the base on which we build the sample lessons in Chapters 4–6.

Situated Cognition: A Theory of Learning

Situated Cognition is a learning theory that assumes all knowledge is situated in actions that occur within cultural, social, and physical contexts (Collins, Brown, & Holum, 1991). That is a very fancy way of saying that knowledge is inseparable from doing. More importantly, knowledge cannot be separated from the means in which the knowledge is learned *by the community that "knows" it*. In our case, situated cognition tells us that students *can only understand* science ideas if they understand how the practice of science leads to those ideas.

If we tell a small child that the stove is hot and will burn her, does that child now "understand" the concepts of heat and burning? They might not touch the stove because they were told not to, but they haven't truly developed an understanding without also learning how the knowledge of "stove = danger" came into being. We've separated the knowledge from the process of gaining the knowledge.

Similarly, we can tell students that the mitochondria is the "battery of the cell." They can then repeat this on an exam, and label it properly as the squiggly-bit on the picture. But, do those students now truly understand what the mitochondria is and does?

Situated cognition tells us that true knowing doesn't happen without action. How do we find out what the mitochondria does? Maybe we lack the resources to gather our own evidence in the classroom, but what evidence can we draw on? These are actions. Fundamentally, situated cognition tells us that knowing is a verb, not a noun, as opposed to theories of knowledge as accumulated stuff in our brains (Greeno, 1994). From the last chapter, we now know that students think science knowledge is stuff to remember. Scientists think science knowledge is the result of doing science. The way scientists view science was already consistent with situated cognition before anyone even coined the term.

We spent the first chapter talking about how scientists do science for a very important reason. When we discussed the science practices and performance expectations, we saw how the NGSS tightly integrates science practice and science content. The NGSS was designed based on the *Framework*, which itself was based on the research done in situated cognition theory and application (National Research Council, 2012). This becomes obvious when we look back at how the NGSS performance expectations are written:

Students who demonstrate understanding can

1. Construct an argument supported by empirical evidence to support . . . [content]
2. Develop a model based on evidence to illustrate . . . [content]
3. Analyze and interpret data on the . . . [content]
4. Construct, use, and present arguments to support the claim that . . . [content]
5. Conduct an investigation to provide evidence that . . . [content]

(You might notice I keep showing you this. That's because it's important!) Here's the general formula:

Students who demonstrate understanding . . . can perform science practice . . . in pursuit of content

Situated cognition says that students *can only understand* science ideas if they understand how to practice science in context. Merely "knowing" some science fact does not in itself signify understanding, no more than being able to repeat that the stove is hot signifies understanding of hotness. It should be clear that the NGSS as a set of standards presupposes the validity of situated cognition as a model for how students come to understand science. This makes situated cognition the ideal framework on which to start the construction of our understanding of how to teach science practice.

Students learn science by doing science. This theory of learning leads to the obvious theory of teaching: You teach students science by teaching them how to do science and then having them do it. This is what we call cognitive apprenticeship, and it is the polar opposite of teaching-by-telling.

Cognitive Apprenticeship: A Theory of Teaching

In a traditional apprenticeship, the apprentice learns processes through physical integration into the practices associated with the content area (Pratt, 1998). As an example from my own past, I once trained as an electrician's apprentice before going to college. I worked side-by-side with a professional master electrician who showed me the trade. I learned by watching an expert, then doing electrical work under the supervision of the expert. As I gained more and more abilities, the master electrician allowed me more and more freedom to work until I was eventually practicing on my own. I actually never made it to that final stage. I decided to become a science teacher, instead. However, what do you think student teaching is? Traditional apprenticeship.

Cognitive apprenticeship borrows from traditional apprenticeship as an applied teaching technique for students constrained to the classroom. For example, when we teach science in the classroom using cognitive apprenticeship as a framework, we are really doing what is called *simulated* apprenticeship. Instead, if we get students involved in real science explorations, such as working in a research laboratory on a university campus or research center under the direction of a professional scientist, then the student is doing what Barb and Hay (2001) loosely describe as "science at the elbows of experts."

In this book, we will focus on you, the teacher, developing *simulated* apprenticeship activities to use in the classroom to prepare you and your students for assessment via the NGSS. Fundamentally, though, you will be doing the same thing my master electrician did for me: modeling how science is done, coaching students as they do science, and slowly removing yourself from the process as students gain proficiency (scaffolding).

This is the same thing your master teacher did for you when you were a student teacher.

The framework of cognitive apprenticeship is ideal for teaching science practice due to its foundation in situated cognition theory, as discussed, with its heavy focus on integrating the practice of the expert with the content. Research across many different disciplines has shown that simulating expert-like practice in context and in an aided environment can increase student abilities in an unaided setting (Ghefaili, 2003). Which for us means: creating scientists!

The principal teaching methods of cognitive apprenticeship are summarized in Table 2.2 (Brown, Collins, & Duguid, 1989). *Modeling, coaching,* and *scaffolding* are the principal teaching methods for cognitive apprenticeship. They are designed to help students construct a conceptual model for science content and develop a set of cognitive abilities through the practice of science. *Reflection* and *articulation* serve to internalize the student's observations and experience, as well as aid in integrating new knowledge and problem-solving skills. Finally, *exploration* fosters independence and encourages autonomous problem formulations and solutions.

TABLE 2.2 THE PRINCIPAL METHODS OF COGNITIVE APPRENTICESHIP (BROWN, COLLINS, & DUGUID, 1989).

Method	Description
Modeling	A subject expert explicitly demonstrates a task to the student. The student is able to build a conceptual model for the task. Implicit processes are exposed so that the student can observe and understand the rationale for the process.
Coaching	The expert observes the student attempting a task and gives them feedback and assistance at critical moments. Students are actively involved in the process and are required to integrate sub-abilities and conceptual knowledge.
Scaffolding	The expert assists the student in performing a task, specifically in areas where the student's abilities are still novice-like. Assistance is slowly withdrawn as the student gains new abilities and can manage more of the task on their own.
Reflection	The student reflects on their own performance in solving a problem through analysis and deconstruction. The student can increase their self-awareness of knowledge and compare their own understanding and performance with that of their peers and the expert.
Articulation	The student thinks about his or her own actions and explains them to others, making their knowledge explicit. This allows students to reorganize their knowledge and generalize its application to related problems.
Exploration	In exploration, students investigate new methods, strategies, and test new hypotheses by exploring the problem. Students can set their own goals and develop their own testing strategies, all of which fosters independent learning.

In the typical inquiry-based science lesson, the first three methods are often present, with poor implementations forgetting to incorporate the others. We'll learn that although this may help lead to learning gains in content knowledge, reflection, articulation, and exploration are critically important for gaining science practice abilities. They don't happen on their own in the science classroom. They must be explicitly incorporated into your instruction. In my electrician's apprenticeship, it was similarly important that I reflect on my learning, since I often worked in environments that could kill me! You don't have similar such pre-existing motivation for reflection in your classroom.

Cognitive Apprenticeship in the Classroom

So what might cognitive apprenticeship look like in the science classroom, and how would it compare to the traditional classroom? Reif and Larkin (1991) point out that formal schooling in science typically does not resemble the actual practice of science by scientists. We need to change that! Table 2.3 describes the difference between the traditional classroom and a classroom environment built around the teaching theory of cognitive apprenticeship, which I call *authentic science activities* (Barab & Hay, 2001).

The big points for us are that to teach students science practice, we need to have students do science with proper guidance, work on authentic

TABLE 2.3 A COMPARISON OF TRADITIONAL SCIENCE CLASSROOM ACTIVITIES WITH ACTIVITIES BASED ON COGNITIVE APPRENTICESHIP.

Traditional Science Activities	Authentic Science Activities
Students *listen* to a teacher tell them how others do science.	Students *do* science in context to answer real questions.
Knowledge and practice are *presented as facts*.	Knowledge and practice are found to be *tentative*, *context based*, and *socially negotiated*.
Learning occurs by *reading* the pages of textbooks and by *listening* to teachers.	Learning occurs while *doing* science with proper guidance.
Problems have classroom applications, but not necessarily real-world applications.	Problems are *authentic* and in response to real-world needs.
Students *hear* about scientific communities.	Students *participate* in a scientific community.
Students rarely reflect on their work or evaluate their own learning.	Students are presented with multiple formal opportunities and support for *reflection and self-evaluation*.

Source: Adapted from Barab and Hay (2001).

problems with real-world connections, work collaboratively with peers and experts, and reflect on their learning. This covers all of the key methods in cognitive apprenticeship outlined in Table 2.2, and all of the classroom necessities for authentic science learning outlined in Table 2.3.

Inquiry and Cognitive Apprenticeship

Inquiry-based learning is a pedagogical technique compatible with cognitive apprenticeship where lessons are framed as a question, a problem, or some sort of investigation, as opposed to the teaching-by-telling process of descriptions and/or explanations of "facts." Fundamentally, inquiry is a "constructivist" pedagogy, where students construct their own knowledge and make meaning of it based on personal experiences (Bachtold, 2013). Students actively participate in the development of the new knowledge by participating in authentic activities (Roth & Jornet, 2013).

Heather Banchi and Randy Bell outline the four levels of inquiry, which I have provided for you in Table 2.4 (Banchi & Bell, 2008). In the same table, I also show how these ideas of inquiry seamlessly integrate with the principle teaching techniques in cognitive apprenticeship of modeling, coaching, scaffolding, and exploration. The levels of inquiry progress from completely teacher-supplied exploration, where the research question, science practices, procedure, and result are all given, to complete open exploration, where the student supplies all of these things.

TABLE 2.4 HOW THE LEVELS OF INQUIRY WITHIN INQUIRY-BASED LEARNING FIT WITHIN THE FRAMEWORK OF COGNITIVE APPRENTICESHIP. THE LEVELS OF INQUIRY ARE TAKEN FROM BANCHI AND BELL (2008).

Methods in Cognitive Apprenticeship	Levels of Inquiry
Modeling	*Confirmation inquiry*: The teacher develops an activity that uses science practice to guide the student to the discovery of already known content.
Coaching	*Structured inquiry*: The teacher provides a question, the science practice to be used, and possibly the procedure that guides the student to discover new content.
Scaffolding	*Guided inquiry*: The teacher provides only the question, expecting the student to decide on the proper practices and specific procedures. Assistance is provided and slowly removed.
Exploration	*Open exploration*: The student provides the research question, the science practices to be used, and the procedure.

Like in cognitive apprenticeship, Banchi and Bell (2008) state that inquiry should proceed along these levels, only moving up as the student gains competence. In the same way, our electrician's apprentice starts by watching the master, then is allowed to practice under strict supervision, with the apprentice eventually being able to do his or her own troubleshooting with slowly decreasing master supervision, until finally the apprentice can practice completely on his or her own, from defining the problem to executing a solution.

We see that inquiry-based learning is a method in science teaching that fits nicely within cognitive apprenticeship. Cognitive apprenticeship is an excellent framework for science teaching because it focuses specifically on the practices of the expert and working with the student so that they develop those expert-like practices. And finally, cognitive apprenticeship as a theory of teaching is ideally suited for the view that students only truly understand when integrating practice with content, which is what situated cognition and the *Framework* on which the NGSS were built tell us.

There is a lot of information out there for teachers on using inquiry in their science classrooms. The examples that follow in Chapters 4–6 will be further such examples. However, I want to be very clear: Doing hands-on science in the classroom is not all it takes for students to be doing inquiry-based learning within the framework of cognitive apprenticeship. Not all inquiry-based lessons are good cognitive apprenticeship. As we found in the first chapter, if all we do is keep our students confined to the first level (confirmation inquiry), then we can easily speak directly to their existing novice-like views about science. Also, if we approach inquiry as merely a process to teach and reinforce content, which is possible, then even though our activities might be considered inquiry, we are not doing cognitive apprenticeship.

Is Modeling, Coaching, and Scaffolding Enough to Teach Science Practice?

It is clear that getting students involved in actively constructing knowledge works for teaching content, but the evidence is beginning to suggest that we must do more to teach practice. Surprisingly, even "doing" science through inquiry methods is not necessarily sufficient for a student to learn how science is done! To do that, we have to ensure that our activities encompass all of the methods of cognitive apprenticeship laid out in Table 2.2, not just modeling, coaching, and scaffolding. Those weird people like you and me that I described in the introduction to this book may be able to synthesize a good practice framework from doing simulated science in the classroom, but for the large majority of your students, that same synthesis just doesn't happen without explicit instruction and reflection.

For some evidence of this, I want to point you to some of my own research. During the development of a physical science course for pre-service elementary and middle school teachers in Virginia, my research group "accidentally" discovered that best practices with respect to learning gains in content knowledge can fail to result in measurable gains in scientific reasoning and practice abilities (Moore, 2012; Moore & Rubbo, 2012). The course we designed was built completely around a research-verified guided-inquiry curriculum with no lecture component, where students participated in 100% hands-on laboratory activities each and every day. The class was a lot of fun for the students and for the instructor (me!). This group of pre-service teachers were learning science by "doing" science. But did they learn how to think like a scientist? Did they learn the practices necessary to do science on their own?

Figure 2.1 shows students' gains in learning as measured by several different assessments (Hake, 1998; Moore & Rubbo, 2012). The three assessments were on content knowledge in circuits, content knowledge

Figure 2.1 Student learning gains as measured by two content assessments (circuits and motion) and one cognitive assessment (scientific reasoning). The average learning gain achieved for traditionally taught courses in the two content areas is roughly 25%. For more details, see Moore (2012) and Moore and Rubbo (2012).

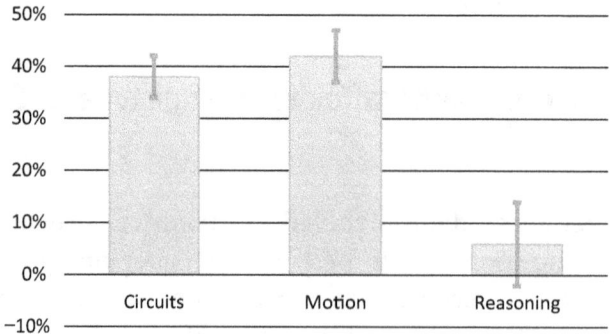

in kinematics, and the Lawson's Classroom Test for Scientific Reasoning (LCTSR). Twenty-five percent roughly represents the learning gain an average student would achieve in the content areas through "traditional" lecture-based instruction. My students demonstrated substantial gains in content knowledge, well above what would be expected from the traditional classroom; however, I measured no demonstrable increase in science thinking abilities. Inquiry alone failed me and my students!

This same general theme is found in several other studies across multiple disciplines. For example, Barbara White and John Frederiksen (1998) found that middle school students studying physical science through an inquiry-based approach did measurably improve on content-based knowledge assessments. However, when students were assessed on their understanding of the inquiry process (science practice), these students demonstrated little improvement. Lisa Blank (2000) found that seventh-grade students studying ecology through a research-based pedagogy did gain an above-average knowledge of content, albeit with little to no corresponding "restructuring of their ecology understandings."

What is it that we are missing, then, if so-called doing science doesn't necessarily improve a student's ability to do science? Within the cognitive apprenticeship framework, students *should* be acquiring understanding of how experts do science by doing simulated science in an expert-like way. But that understanding doesn't necessarily materialize for most students (maybe just the "weird" ones). What is it we must do in our instruction, then, to prepare students for NGSS practice-based performance expectations?

Biology teachers Thomas Lord and Terri Orkwiszewski (2006) nicely sum up the issue in the following quote:

> Involving students in inquiry-based exercises is much more difficult than simply providing activities for them to do in the classroom. While active learning suggests students are physically participating in the lesson, inquiry learning requires that they are also mentally participating in it. Academic theorists agree it is more the mental participation than the physical participation that is the important ingredient to enduring understanding.

Let's go back to the normal student and the weird student I discussed in the introduction. The weird students loves science. When they get involved in an inquiry-based activity, they don't just physically participate, but they actively engage mentally in all aspects of the activity. They want to know why they are doing what they are doing, how what they are doing will get them the knowledge they want, how the activity could be generalized for future use in other areas, and they think about their own thinking and the ways it can be improved. That weird student picks up on the practices because they are motivated and metacognitively aware enough to do so. As a science educator, *you're* weird. The entire metacognitive process just happens in your head automatically, so it's easy for you to assume it naturally happens in your students' heads. It doesn't.

As we learned in Chapter 1, one of the defining differences between the science expert and novice is what Deanna Kuhn (2004) calls an "epistemological appreciation" of how new knowledge is formed. The major distinction between the novice and the expert is in the way they think about and view science and its practice. The expert consistently evaluates his or her own thinking and utilizes multiple resources toward solving a problem, making an observation, coming up with a hypothesis, and conducting experiments. The novice is typically "stuck" in one type of framing and rarely evaluates their own reasoning. Therefore, we find that metacognition, the simple act of thinking about thinking, is also a defining practice of the expert scientist.

In fact, Eugenia Etkina and Jose Mestre (2004) identify the importance of metacognition as one of the key, defining insights about the student that we can get from science education research. Specifically, when the science instruction the student is receiving doesn't fit the student's mental model for what science is, then it becomes easy for them to disengage from the course, believing that what they are doing is not important to learning. If the student expects to passively receive facts, as we've seen they do from Table 1.1 in the previous chapter, then the guided-inquiry activity can seem to them like play-time that doesn't really hurt, but doesn't necessarily lead to any real learning about science.

Somehow, we need to get the student "in the game." It's not enough for the student to physically participate in the act of doing science. They have to mentally reflect on what it is they are doing in order to see how the practice itself is the means by which we know this stuff to be true. That means that you, the teacher, need to guide them not only through the activity, but through the thinking. If you want your students to become mentally engaged, and not just physically engaged, then you have to get students to buy-in to what it is they are doing in the classroom.

Be Explicit. Be Reflective. Make It Count.

As discussed earlier, White and Frederiksen found little improvement in the science practice abilites of their middle school physical science students using an inquiry-based approach. However, when they added a significant metacognitive component to instruction that they call "Reflective Assessment," students perfromed significantly better on an assessment of practice, with the greatest effect observed for low-achieving students (White & Frederiksen, 1998). Similarly, Blank (2000) showed that incorporating discussions on the metacognitive aspects of the lesson improved the understanding of practice in ecology among middle school biology students.

In my own research, we found that making science thinking patterns explicit during instruction and including significant formal opportunities for students to reflect on their practice both during and after activities has resulted in significant improvement in science thinking. We kept using the same inquiry-based activities, we just added to them. Figure 2.2 shows learning gains in science reasoning for students in classes without and with the explicit/reflective components (Moore, 2012). What's most interesting is that both groups of students participated in essentially the same activities. The first group could get away with physical participation, but not necessarily full mental participation. The second group was guided through both physical and mental participation.

It appears that explicit instruction in thinking is really necessary for teaching practices effectively. Biologist Anton Lawson makes clear the necessity to be explicit in instruction of scientific reasoning, specifically

Figure 2.2 Incorporating explicit reasoning instruction, reflective exercises, and assessment on science thinking led to significant improvement in students' scientific reasoning abilities.

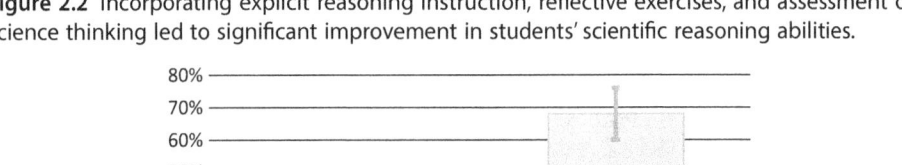

when having students design experiments to test hypotheses (Lawson, 2000). From an excellent review of the research on learning, Etkina and Mestre (2004) identify several instructional principles, one of which is the explicit teaching of metacognitive strategies so that students learn how to learn.

Table 2.5 shows a summary of the nine instructional principles Etkina and Mestre (2004) were able to synthesize from the available research in science teaching and learning. I have broken these principles down into three easy to remember categories:

1. Be explicit.
2. Be reflective.
3. Make it count.

The research is fairly clear on this: In order for students to pick up on the practices you have them doing in your activities, you must be explicit about what it is that they are doing. Tell them what practice they are going to use, show them how to use that practice, and guide them in their execution. Both during and after the activity, students need to reflect on what it is they are doing. It is your job to ensure this is happening. And finally, students need to believe that what they are doing matters. Therefore, you must make it very clear to students that you find the execution of practices to be important. You can tell them this, but the best way is to show them

TABLE 2.5 THE NINE INSTRUCTIONAL PRINCIPLES ETKINA AND MESTRE (2004) IDENTIFY FROM A REVIEW OF RESEARCH IN SCIENCE TEACHING AND LEARNING. I HAVE BROKEN THESE PRINCIPLES DOWN INTO THREE EASY TO REMEMBER CATEGORIES.

Be explicit.	♦ "Metacognitive strategies should be taught so that students learn how to learn." ♦ "Helping students organize content knowledge according to some hierarchy should be a priority."
Be reflective.	♦ "Construction and sense-making of science knowledge should be encouraged." ♦ "Qualitative reasoning based on concepts should be encouraged." ♦ "Hypothetico-deductive reasoning should be encouraged." ♦ "Ample opportunities should be available for learning 'the processes of doing science.'"
Make it count.	♦ "Formative assessment should be used frequently to monitor students' understanding and to help tailor instruction to meet students' needs." ♦ "Ample opportunities should be provided for students to apply their knowledge flexibly across multiple contexts." ♦ "Motivation is an important factor."

by making practices count. That is to say, make practices at least as important to their grade as content knowledge.

Successfully Implementing Cognitive Apprenticeship in the Classroom

We've weaved our way through some interesting research to come to a pretty clear understanding of what it takes to get your teaching and students' attention focused on science practice. Inquiry alone is not enough, since we have to deal with the metacognitive aspect of learning, especially when it comes to science practices. Table 2.6 summarizes the distinction between a poor approach to inquiry and a good approach.

In poor executions of inquiry-based teaching, it is assumed that students will automatically pick up on the practices being used simply by doing them. However, the research tells us that you need to be *explicit about the practices* that are being used, explain their utility, and model their effective use for students to start actually learning science practice.

During poor inquiry activities, both the instructor and the student focus on completing the activity and getting a satisfactory result, where the result is typically some known "fact." However, a focus on results-as-facts or experiments-as-verification, as we saw in Chapter 1, can result in the reinforcement of novice science views and practices. The data tell us that you

TABLE 2.6 WHAT A POOR, NON-AUTHENTIC APPROACH TO INQUIRY LOOKS LIKE, AND HOW IT COMPARES TO AN AUTHENTIC APPROACH BASED ON COGNITIVE APPRENTICESHIP.

Non-Authentic Inquiry Activities	Authentic Inquiry Activities
It is assumed that students will *automatically pick up* on the practices being used simply by doing them.	The instructor is *explicit about the practices* that are being used, explains their utility, and models their effective use.
The instructor and student focus on completing the activity and *getting a satisfactory result*.	The instructor facilitates *reflection-in-action* through all stages by encouraging the student to focus on the practices instead of the result.
Students *compare their result to some known fact*, and both the instructor and student are generally satisfied if the result is roughly consistent with the fact.	Students compare their result with that of their peers in the community of practice. The instructor facilitates *reflection-on-action* and is satisfied if the student demonstrates good practice.
The use of science practice *is confined to the activity*. The instructor and the student do not expect the student to independently demonstrate good practice in the future.	The instructor clearly expects the student to be able to independently utilize the practices from the activity in the future in a different context. The student's performance is *made to count*.

must facilitate reflection through all stages by encouraging students to focus on the practices instead of the result.

And finally, if the use of science practice is confined to the specific activity, and you signal to students that they will not be expected to independently demonstrate good practice in the future, then students will rightfully discount the activity. You must be clear with students that they are expected to learn science practices and that their performance will be made to count.

A Checklist for Quality Practice-Centric Activities

Now, let's take everything that we have learned in this chapter and distill it down to a simple research-verified framework of generative principles for you to use in creating or modifying activities that focus on science practices. I've provided the checklist in Table 2.7 along with descriptions of each item. The checklist is summarized as follows:

- Choose or design an activity that allows students to construct knowledge about the content to be learned through one or more science practices.
- Build a community of practice in the classroom that supports the activity. Students should work on teams and teams should communicate with other teams. As the expert, you need to be right in the middle of the activity, too.
- Be explicit about the practices and reasoning patterns needed during the activity.
- Facilitate reflection on the practices both during and after the activity.
- Make it obvious to the student that the practice and process is as important as or more important than the specific content knowledge gained. Reinforce this in your grading.

We will talk about "making it count" in more detail in the next chapter, where we will use the research on assessing science practice to figure out a way to assess our students both in the moment and after. In Chapters 4–6, we will look at specific examples of activities built with this checklist for practices within the dimensions of investigation, interpretation, and

TABLE 2.7 A CHECKLIST FOR DEVELOPING ACTIVITIES THAT EFFECTIVELY TEACH SCIENCE PRACTICES, BASED ON THE RESEARCH ON LEARNING AND TEACHING. EXAMPLES OF PUTTING THIS CHECKLIST INTO PRACTICE ARE PROVIDED IN LATER CHAPTERS.

Checklist	Description
Identify the practice and content	What practice or practices will be used in the activity to learn what content? Ideally, format this within the structure of the NGSS performance expectations, either by using one of the expectations exactly, or creating a new one in a similar format.
Identify how the student will construct knowledge	What is the specific approach you will take with instruction? Clearly define the primary method used, such as *modeling, coaching, scaffolding,* or *exploration*.
Define the community the student will work within	How will individual students work within a small community? How will that small community interact with the larger classroom community? Is there writing with peer review? Communication in simulated conferences? Formal opportunities for argument from evidence?
Define the explicit instruction to be given	What is going to be made explicit? You need to clearly state what science practices and reasoning patterns you will highlight through explicit instruction, such as: "now, we are doing, . . . which allows us to know . . ."
Identify how you will encourage reflection	At what points in the activity will you probe individual students? The group? The class? What explicit opportunities will you take to facilitate reflection on- and in-action?
Define how the activity will be made to count	How will you make it obvious to the student that the practice and process is important? How will the activity be graded? What will the student be expected to do from this activity in the future for a summative grade?

communication, respectively. And finally, in Chapter 7, I will show you the step-by-step process we used to design a practice-based lesson based on this checklist as well as how to use the checklist to take an off-the-shelf lesson and turn it into a science practice-teaching machine. You can use this same process to start building and/or modifying your own lessons for the content in your course.

Imagine What Would Happen if . . .

I want you to imagine what would happen if you started each and every day in your class showing your students the eight science practices defined in the NGSS performance expectations. At the beginning of each activity, you remind them that this is what scientists do and that this is what you expect them to be able to do in order to succeed in your class.

After you reintroduce the eight science practices, you introduce a new activity on some interesting new content. You tell the students that they are going to explore this area by using one or more of the science practices. They get their hands dirty with some fun activity, learn a few context-dependent skills along the way, and discover for themselves some interesting new aspect of science.

During the activity, you ask the students probing questions about their thinking: What does this tell you? How do you know that? Why is your data a little different from this other group's data? You point out those practices during the activity, keeping your students focused on completing the task in an expert-like way, and forcing them to think about what they're doing.

After the activity, you have student groups present their results and compare with their classmates. With the whole class, you point to the practices once again and ask: Which of these practices did you use? How could you use this practice in another context? Why does this tell you something interesting about the world?

And finally, when it comes time to assign a grade, you assess your students on the science practices. Not just on whether or not they can remember them, but whether or not they can use them. Will those students start taking the practices in your class seriously? Will they buy-in to the instruction if they are graded on those things you focus on in class? Yes. They will.

Now I want you to imagine one more thing. Imagine that this same scene plays out in the same way during their biology, chemistry, earth science, and physical science lessons. Imagine this same scene plays out in the same way in second grade, fifth grade, ninth grade, and their senior year in high school. Do you think that by the time they graduate, they will know the science practices? Do you think that by the time they graduate that they will understand the cross-cutting nature of the scientific method? Do you think they will have a significantly greater appreciation for the process of science and have a deeper understanding of what science is as opposed to science as facts?

You better believe they will! That is the power of being explicit, being reflective, and making it count.

Summary

In this chapter, I have tried to answer the question, How do we teach science practice? To this end, we have discussed situated cognition as a theory of learning, cognitive apprenticeship as a theory of teaching, and how classroom-based activities can be built from this framework, typically referred to as inquiry-based lessons. The methods necessary for good practice-centric lessons were *modeling, coaching, scaffolding, reflection, articulation,* and *exploration.*

Unfortunately, we learned that simply pulling pre-made inquiry-based lessons off the shelf and deploying them in our classrooms doesn't necessarily lead to much learning with respect to science practices if we are not careful. We examined a great deal of research that shows that to adequately teach practices and reasoning abilities, we have to *be explicit, be reflective,* and *make practices count.* This walk through the research allowed us to build a simple checklist for our activities that help ensure that students will learn what it is that we want them to learn.

The following is a brief summary of the main points:

- Getting students actively constructing their own knowledge leads to greater content knowledge learning and retention.
- Methods of cognitive apprenticeship are modeling, coaching, scaffolding, reflection, articulation, and exploration.
- Well-designed inquiry-based methods and activities are proven to improve student learning and are fun and enjoyable for the student.
- It's not enough for students to physically participate in the activities, but they must also mentally participate.
- This requires you to do the following during the activities:
    - Be explicit about the practice and thinking needed for the activity.
    - Be reflective about those practices and thinking both during and after the activity.
    - Make it count by making it clear that the practice and thinking are at least equally as important as the content.

References

Bachtold, M. (2013). What do students "construct" according to constructivism in science education? *Research in Science Education, 43,* 2477–2496.

Banchi, H., & Bell, R. (2008). The many levels of inquiry. *Science and Children, 46*(2), 26–29.

Barab, S., & Hay, K. (2001). Doing science at the elbows of experts: Issues related to the science apprenticeship camp. *Journal of Research in Science Teaching, 38*(1), 70–102.

Blank, L. M. (2000). A metacognitive learning cycle: A better warranty for student understanding? *Science Education, 84*(4), 486–506.

Brown, J., Collins, A., & Duguid, P. (1989). Situated cognition and the culture of learning. *Educational Researcher, 18,* 32.

Collins, A., Brown, J., & Holum, A. (1991). Cognitive apprenticeship: Making thinking visible. *American Educator, 6,* 38–46.

Etkina, E., & Mestre, J. P. (2004). Implications of learning research for teaching science to non-science majors. In *SENCER* (pp. 1–26). Harrisburg, PA. Retrieved from http://ncsce.net/implications-of-learning-research-for-teaching-science-to-non-science-majors/

Ghefaili, A. (2003). Cognitive apprenticeship, technology, and the contextualization of learning environments. *Journal of Educational Computing, Design, and Online Learning, 4,* 1–27.

Greeno, J. (1994). Gibson's affordances. *Psychological Review, 101*(2), 336–342.

Hake, R. R. (1998). Interactive-engagement vs traditional methods: A six-thousand student survey of mechanics test data for introductory physics courses. *American Journal of Physics, 66,* 64–74.

Kuhn, D. (2004). What is scientific thinking and how does it develop? In U. Goswami (Ed.), *Blackwell Handbook of Childhood Cognitive Development* (pp. 371–393). Malden, MA: Wiley-Blackwell.

Lawson, A. E. (2000). The generality of hypothetico-deductive reasoning: Making scientific thinking explicit. *American Biology Teacher, 62,* 482.

Lord, T., & Orkwiszewski, T. (2006). Moving from didactic to inquiry-based instruction in a science laboratory. *The Biology Teacher, 68*(6), 342–345.

Moore, J. C. (2012). Transitional to formal operational: Using authentic research experiences to get non-science students to think more like scientists. *European Journal of Physics Education, 3*(4), 1–12.

Moore, J. C., & Rubbo, L. J. (2012). Scientific reasoning abilities of nonscience majors in physics-based courses. *Physical Review Special Topics—Physics Education Research*, *8*, 010106.

National Research Council. (2012). *A Framework for K–12 Science Education: Practices, Crosscutting Concepts, and Core Ideas*. Washington, DC: The National Academies Press.

Papert, S. (1991). Situating constructionism. In I. Harel & S. Papert (Eds.), *Constructionism: Research Reports and Essays* (pp. 1–11). Norwood, NJ: Ablex.

Pratt, D. (1998). *Five Perspectives on Teaching in Adult and Higher Education*. Malabar, FL: Krieger Publishing Company.

Reif, F., & Larkin, J. (1991). Cognition in scientific and everyday domains: Comparisons and learning implications. *Journal of Research in Science Teaching*, *28*, 733–760.

Roth, W.-M., & Jornet, A. (2013). Toward a theory of experience. *Science Education*, *98*(1), 106–126.

White, B. Y., & Frederiksen, J. R. (1998). Inquiry, modeling, and metacognition: Making science accessible to all students. *Cognition and Instruction*, *16*(1), 3–118.

3

How Do You Assess Science Practice?

"Students can hit any target that they know about and that holds still for them."
—*Stiggins and Chappuis* (2017)

In the last chapter, we talked about the importance of making science practices "count." In this chapter, we'll discuss how to do that. We'll focus on how to monitor and assess students in their deployment of science practices. We'll also discuss how to build an assessable curriculum, since assessment is obviously tied to what we define as our learning goals. What are those goals, what will we do in the classroom to achieve those goals, and how will we know whether or not we were successful?

The main point of this chapter centers on the quote at the beginning:

> "Students can hit any target that they know about and that holds still for them."

We'll discuss those targets in the context of the *Framework*, the Next Generation Science Standards (NGSS), and the research, how we can communicate those targets to the student, how we can build lessons that provide the student with the necessary practice at aiming for those targets, and how we can measure the student's ability to hit those targets.

To this end, we'll first discuss how to design a curriculum. Specifically, we'll take a generic framework for curriculum development and assessment and apply it to creating and assessing lessons that combine practice and content in the context of the NGSS. I will describe how you can use the NGSS's Disciplinary Core Ideas (DCIs) and performance expectations to set learning goals. Then, we'll look at how to build a learning experience in the classroom based on those goals, and how to use the NGSS "evidence statements" to assess practices and content knowledge together. Which traditional strategies work and which fail? What would practice-centric tests look like? How do you assess actions as opposed to knowledge? Finally, I'll discuss the importance of communicating your goals and assessment strategies to your students, and re-evaluating everything based on their feedback.

Curriculum and Assessment: A Framework for Making It Count

Assessment is integrated with curriculum. Assessment implies that you have first identified what you want your students to be able to do. What is it that you want the student to learn? You must first answer this question before thinking about what specific assessment strategies you should use. Thankfully, broad-view learning goals are clearly laid out for us in the NGSS.

After defining goals, we can only then begin to build specific learning activities and assessments that achieve and measure the understanding we seek. Sometimes, we may determine how we want to assess the student after we've decided on what they will do in the classroom, and sometimes specific activities can be built based on pre-determined assessment strategies. Occasionally, we learn during assessment that the activities we did design failed miserably to foster understanding. It's also possible that we observe understanding even when our assessments tell us otherwise, which may indicate the need to re-evaluate the assessment.

Finally, it is critically important that we communicate to students exactly what we expect of them, and how we intend to assess them. This last part is the critical component in the "making it count" portion of our framework for teaching science practice described in the last chapter. They need to know their "target."

Table 3.1 shows the basic framework we will use to lay out an assessable curriculum, which also serves as the guide for the rest of the chapter. Specifically, to assess practice abilities, you will need to do the following:

- identify learning goals;
- align the curriculum with those goals;
- create both formative and summative assessments;
- communicate those learning goals to the student; and
- re-evaluate everything based on student feedback and classroom experience.

I would like to point out that the generic framework shown in Table 3.1 is not specific to designing practice-based activities and associated assessments in science. In fact, for those of you that are in-service teachers, it should look roughly familiar since it is exactly the same research-based framework we would expect to use for curriculum development in any context.

In particular, when done correctly, the development of assessment and curriculum go hand-in-hand. To assess science practice, you must first know how to build a curriculum that incorporates science practice. To that end, I'll briefly describe two approaches from the research literature on curriculum development and their implications for assessment: (1) product-based, and (2) process-based curriculum (Smith, 2000). Then, I'll show you how you can use this research to structure your thinking about what to do in your own classes. In the following sections, we'll look at examples.

TABLE 3.1 A FRAMEWORK FOR BUILDING AN ASSESSABLE PRACTICE-BASED CURRICULUM.

Task	Description
Identify learning goals	What is it that you want the student to understand?
Align curriculum with goals	How can you build a curriculum that achieves this understanding?
Create assessments	How will you evaluate whether not the student understands?
Communicate goals	How are you communicating to students what they are expected to understand by the end of the course/lesson?
Re-evaluate	How will you know if your curriculum is working?

The traditional product-based curriculum development theorist Ralph Tyler (1949) describes a systematic framework for developing learning, where learning objectives are set, a plan of action is determined and put into place, and the "products" are measured. Curriculum theorist Hilda Taba (1962) synthesized a procedure for product-based curriculum development as follows:

Step 1: Diagnosis of need
Step 2: Formulation of objectives
Step 3: Selection of content
Step 4: Organization of content
Step 5: Selection of learning experiences
Step 6: Organization of learning experiences
Step 7: Determination of what to evaluate and of the ways and means of doing it

This procedure looks very similar to the shorter framework shown in Table 3.1, with the obvious omission of the final reflective step. However, like the limited deductive-based scientific method we discussed in Chapter 1, we must also be careful with taking strict procedural approaches to the practice of teaching. In particular, when we set the entire curriculum including assessments before day one of instruction, then we leave the learner out of the process all together. They participate in activities we design, but they have little say in the actual learning process. Furthermore, feedback they provide via assessments plays no role in future instruction. This approach also has the effect of forcing a focus on the individual "products" themselves, instead of a consistent learning experience, which can minimize learning that happens outside of pre-defined products.

As an example, imagine our product is the following NGSS performance expectation (we'll come back to this example in later sections, too):

MS-PS2–5. Conduct an investigation and evaluate the experimental design to provide evidence that fields exist between objects exerting forces on each other even though the objects are not in contact.

A significant amount of learning has to happen leading up to a student being able to demonstrate understanding in the domain of magnetic fields. Maybe a student would develop a taxonomy of materials, including magnetic, ferromagnetic, and non-magnetic materials. How do these different types of materials interact with each other? They might discover that not all metals are ferromagnetic. What "makes" a magnet? What's a compass? All of these ideas would be built into activities leading up to a field model for magnetic interactions. Much of this learning isn't explicitly mentioned in the NGSS. Is this learning less important? If not, then do we just need to add more and more performance expectations to cover everything?

The practical effect of curriculum as products is the breaking down of learning into smaller and smaller units, where the teacher is faced with an avalanche of stuff to teach and assess and little to no flexibility. More recent research shows that curriculums based on products, or strict "learning objectives," are rarely actually implemented in this way, anyway (Cornbleth, 1990). This isn't necessarily a failure of the teacher, but possibly a failure of the framework to align with how learning actually happens. There are interesting parallels between the practice of science and the practice of teaching. The *Framework* and NGSS on which this entire book is written fundamentally lay out science as a process to be practiced. Similarly, the research in curriculum development is also beginning to focus on teaching as a process to be practiced.

Process-based curriculum recognizes learning as an interaction between the teacher and the student, with learning happening in both directions (Stenhouse, 1975). The focus is more on big ideas where the curriculum *is* the interaction, allowing for a more organic learning experience. With respect to the NGSS, the set of DCIs is significantly smaller than would be typical for more "traditional" science standards. Within the NGSS, the main focus is on the interaction between the practices, content, and cross-cutting ideas. This has the practical benefit of having less "stuff" to assess, and when implemented correctly, allows greater flexibility on how that interaction is taught and learned, allowing freedom for student input into the curriculum. This is similar to Ted Wragg's (1997) "cubic curriculum," which has the dimensions of subject matter, cross-curricular themes, and varying methods of teaching/learning, which is becoming more critical as we learn more about teaching to various populations and demographics.

In her book *Curriculum: Product or Praxis?*, Shirley Grundy (1987, p. 105) describes process-based curriculum as follows:

> Critical pedagogy goes beyond situating the learning experience within the experience of the learner: it is a process which takes the

experiences of both the learner and the teacher and, through dialogue and negotiation, recognizes them both as problematic.

If we revisit Chapter 1 of this book, we see science as a socially negotiated process. Chapter 2 examined situated cognition as a theory where learning requires doing, and cognitive apprenticeship has us teach science by getting students to do science. Doing science necessitates negotiation between everyone involved, including teacher/student. It makes sense, then, that we would want to more thoroughly involve our students in the science learning, and even curriculum building processes. Furthermore, we as teachers must accept this two-way negotiation, and recognize that the feedback we get from the student can help us better teach them.

In particular with respect to science, students enter the classroom with their own experiences and mental models for the world around them based on those experiences. Sometimes, their experiences lead to mental models that clash with "correct" models of the world. Specifically, in the mind of the student, the idea that the squished bug on the windshield exerted the same force on the car as the car exerted on it is preposterous. No matter how much we tell the student otherwise, they won't believe us, whether or not they can regurgitate the "fact" on a test.

If we wish to lead them to understanding, we cannot discount these experiences and pre-existing mental models. Their ideas are valid, even if based on limited experiences. In this example, the student has a *different* model in their mind for force, and it isn't an absurd model based on their experiences. The bug *lost*! We must learn from the student how they think and why they think that way, so that we can build learning experiences that lead the student to grow without having to invalidate their own experiences. Sometimes, as teachers, we can anticipate the students' thinking, and sometimes we cannot. When we can't, we need to readjust our own teaching if necessary, and even re-evaluate our learning goals from time to time. This is curriculum as process.

We have to be careful here, though. More than likely the state you work in and/or the school system in which you teach has some pretty specific ideas about what your students should be learning. Within the confines of formal schooling, there is only so much leverage the student has in negotiating learning goals, if any. The NGSS has defined performance expectations that you will have to assess, no matter how many great arguments your students make. There is a great deal of flexibility, but there is also a definite structure.

This is why Table 3.1 takes a hybrid approach to curriculum development, where we are systematic about our goals and the process we go through to develop activities, but we leave open the ability to re-evaluate our own teaching and curriculum decisions based on feedback from students. We have a well-defined plan, but we recognize the need for occasional flexibility. For example, we may have a performance expectation like **MS-PS2–5** discussed above, but we have a great deal of flexibility in how we build a learning progression that gets everyone there, and we have the freedom to go beyond strictly delineated products in the design of that progression.

For the rest of this chapter, we will look at the NGSS as our set of broad-based learning goals and learn to build a curriculum based on these goals using this hybrid approach. Figure 3.1 shows a schematic diagram of the NGSS-based curriculum development process you can use for building your courses, and follows the framework from Table 3.1. Figure 3.1 looks like a funnel, because we get more and more detail and more and more specific as we move down the list.

We start out with the big ideas, break these into smaller sub-ideas, and develop broad performance expectations from these sub-ideas. This sets up our set of learning goals. Then, we decide on a learning progression that could lead a student toward understanding demonstrated by

Figure 3.1 Schematic diagram of a hybrid product/process approach to curriculum development using the NGSS as a guide to defining learning goals.

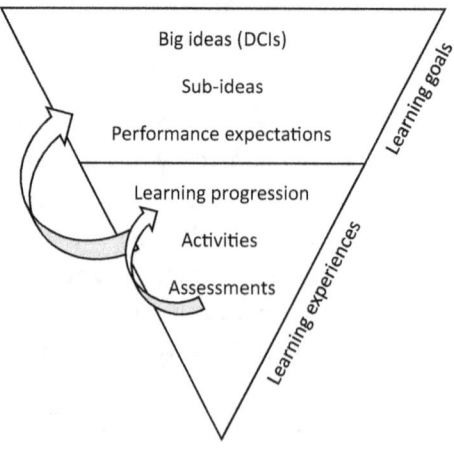

the performance expectation. We create specific activities within that progression, and then we assess performance in those activities. All of these items form the overall learning experience for the student. The arrows in the figure represent the "re-evaluate" task from Table 3.1. Occasionally, we learn during assessment that the activities failed miserably to foster understanding, or that the learning progression was missing pieces. In some cases, assessment can lead us to develop completely new goals.

Identifying What We Want Students to Learn

To demonstrate, let's imagine that we're building a curriculum for middle school physical science. To determine our learning target, we'll first look at the big ideas we want students to learn, then we'll break those big ideas down into manageable sub-ideas, and then determine specific performance expectations we have for students on each of those sub-ideas (as outlined in Figure 3.1). The performance expectations serve as our learning goals and as the foundation of any resulting activities and assessments.

Table 3.2 shows the middle school physical science DCIs from the NGSS with corresponding sub-ideas (NGSS Lead States, 2013a). At the beginning of the academic year when we start thinking about our curriculum, we begin by looking at these four big ideas in physical science. Specifically, the physical science ideas that carry through the grade levels

TABLE 3.2 MIDDLE SCHOOL PHYSICAL SCIENCE DCIS FROM THE NGSS (NGSS LEAD STATES, 2013A).

	Disciplinary Core Ideas	Sub-ideas
MS-PS1	Matter and its Interactions	Structure of matter Chemical reactions
MS-PS2	Forces and Interactions	Forces and motion Types of interactions Stability and instability
MS-PS3	Energy	Definitions of energy Conservation of energy Energy and forces Energy in chemical reactions
MS-PS4	Waves	Wave properties Electromagnetic radiation Information technology

in the NGSS are (1) matter and its interactions, (2) forces, (3) energy, and (4) waves.

Each of the DCIs can be broken down into multiple sub-ideas. Table 3.3 shows the specific sub-ideas and associated performance expectations for *forces and interactions*, as an example (NGSS Lead States, 2013a). At the middle school level, we're interested in students learning about the role of the mass of an object, and how it can be qualitatively accounted for in changes of motion due to forces. Furthermore, we want students to understand field models of forces, and how fields can be mapped by relative strength and effect on objects. As can be seen from the performance expectations, we define understanding through the student's ability to practice science in these specific content domains.

A large-view map of content and its progression throughout the grade levels for each discipline can be found in *Appendix E: Progressions Within the Next Generation Science Standard* (NGSS Lead States, 2013a). When beginning the development of your own curriculum, this is an excellent place to start. I recommend going through the appendix and building your own set of tables similar to Tables 3.2 and 3.3, where one table lays out the big picture (similar to Table 3.2), and several other tables drill down on the specific ideas to address in the classroom through the performance expectations (similar to Table 3.3).

TABLE 3.3 PERFORMANCE EXPECTATIONS FOR DCI MS-PS2, FORCES AND INTERACTIONS. ADAPTED FROM (NGSS LEAD STATES, 2013C).

	Performance Expectations
MS-PS2–1.	Apply Newton's Third Law to *design a solution to a problem* involving the motion of two colliding objects.
MS-PS2–2.	*Plan an investigation* to provide evidence that the change in an object's motion depends on the sum of the forces on the object and the mass of the object.
MS-PS2–3.	*Ask questions* about data to determine the factors that affect the strength of electric and magnetic forces.
MS-PS2–4.	*Construct and present arguments using evidence* to support the claim that gravitational interactions are attractive and depend on the masses of interacting objects.
MS-PS2–5.	*Conduct an investigation* and evaluate the experimental design to provide evidence that fields exist between objects exerting forces on each other even though the objects are not in contact.

Aligning Curriculum With Standards

The DCIs and performance expectations set our goals for learning. In the last section, we used the NGSS to build a map that started with big ideas we want students to understand and narrowed down to specific performance expectations that can demonstrate understanding of those ideas. However, defining what we want students to understand is not yet a complete curriculum. We now must begin to think about the specific learning experiences we want students to go through in the classroom that can lead to the understanding that we seek.

Let's revisit the performance expectation for magnetic fields that we discussed earlier:

> **MS-PS2–5.** Conduct an investigation and evaluate the experimental design to provide evidence that fields exist between objects exerting forces on each other even though the objects are not in contact.

The natural tendency based on a product-view of curriculum would be to immediately begin creating an activity and assessment for this individual performance expectation. However, as we have already discussed, a significant amount of learning has to happen before we can expect the student to understand a concept as abstract as an invisible field. Some of this learning is built into the K–5 curriculum, but not all of it. We need to build a learning progression that guides the student toward a field model of the magnetic force, and ideally revisits learning from previous grade levels.

Table 3.4 shows an example of a possible learning progression for magnets that could lead to an understanding of magnetic fields and more. We start with magnetic interactions, build on that by using compasses to develop a field model for the magnetic force, and then cap learning by exploring magnetic strength based on stacking magnets in various orientations.

Figure 3.2 shows several examples of student work on activities as they move through the learning progression. In Figure 3.2(a), the student is developing a taxonomy of magnetic materials categorized by their interactions with each other. In this particular activity, we used similarly shaped unmarked rods made of different materials that the students played

TABLE 3.4 EXAMPLE LEARNING PROGRESSION FOR MAGNETS.

Ideas	Activities
Magnets and interaction	◆ Taxonomy of interactions for materials ◆ What is different about a magnet and a ferromagnet? ◆ Are all metals magnetic? ◆ Close your eyes, can you tell which object is the magnet?
Abstract models: magnetic fields	◆ A field model for magnets from compass needles—developing a model ◆ Arrangements of magnets and magnetic strength—using a model
Exploration: magnetic strength	◆ Designing an experiment to measure the strength of magnets ◆ Stacking magnets ◆ How does it fit the model we have for magnetic interactions?

Figure 3.2 Example scientific notebook entries for students completing activities in a learning progression on magnets.

(a)

List of Materials
2 metal magnetic rods
wooden rod
brass rod
aluminum rod
plastic rod

Magnetic Pull/Push	Magnetic Pull	Nothing
2 metal steel/iron	aluminum	wood, brass, plastic

Magnets are objects that attract or repel other objects.

Iron (ferro is iron in greek) → Fe

Table to describe interactions

Push + Pull	Pull	none
Push + Pull (sometimes)	Sometimes	none
Nothing	none	none

(b)

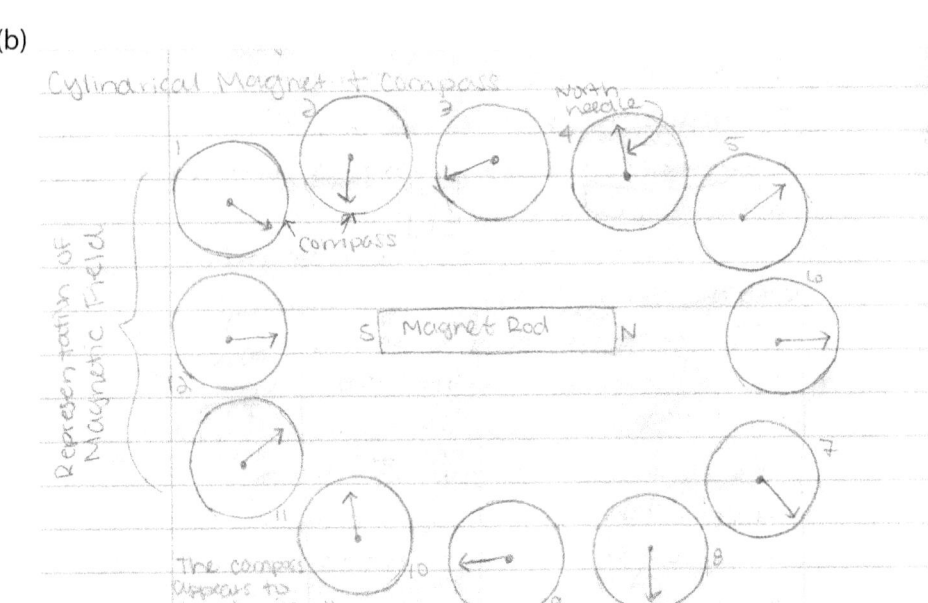

Cylindrical Magnet + Compass

Representation of Magnetic Field

The compass appears to react with the magnet the strongest at north + south poles - the compass needle wiggles less.

(c)

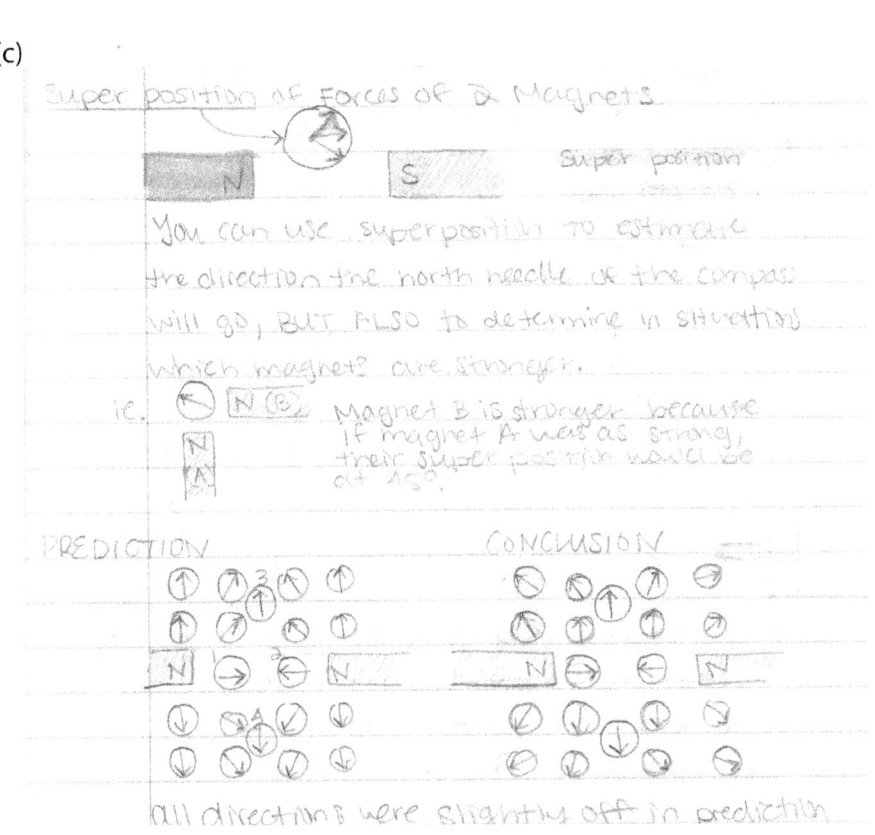

Super position of Forces of 2 Magnets

Super position

You can use superposition to estimate the direction the north needle of the compass will go, BUT ALSO to determine in situations which magnets are stronger.

i.e. Magnet B is stronger because if magnet A was as strong, their superposition would be at 45°.

PREDICTION   CONCLUSION

All directions were slightly off in prediction.

with to discover the various types of interactions. Figure 3.2(b) shows a student having marked the direction of a compass as it was moved around a magnet. Figure 3.2(c) shows a similar activity using multiple magnets, where the student made a prediction using the field model and then they tested that prediction. (I know I'm being terse with respect to these activities. More detailed examples of creating activities in a learning progression are provided in later chapters.)

Some of the content in this learning progression can be explicitly found in the NGSS, while some is nowhere to be seen. For example, in the third grade, magnetic interactions are discussed, as evidenced by the following performance expectation (NGSS Lead States, 2013c):

3-PS2–3. Ask questions to determine cause and effect relationships of electric or magnetic interactions between two objects not in contact with each other.

Students ask questions about magnetic force between two permanent magnets, and/or the force between a magnet and paperclips, and/or the strength of the force exerted by one magnet versus two magnets stacked together. Magnets don't explicitly re-appear in the NGSS until the middle school performance expectation we're using as our example. There is no explicit performance expectation for students using a model for magnetic fields to make predictions about the orientation of a compass needle between multiple magnets, as seen in Figure 3.2(c). That doesn't mean that such an activity is unnecessary. It certainly provides evidence of the existence of fields!

Often misunderstood, the NGSS is a *minimum* set of standards and *not* curriculum. Performance expectations are big-view goals and not products. It's perfectly acceptable and even necessary to expand on both the content and practices described in the NGSS, especially if it helps strengthen student understanding about a topic. Furthermore, it's important for students to utilize as many practices as possible throughout the learning cycle. For example, in the learning progression on magnets that I've shown you in Table 3.4 and Figure 3.2, students could ask questions, develop and use models, conduct investigations, analyze data, use mathematics, construct explanations, argue from evidence, and communicate information, all on the singular topic of magnets. Your classroom instruction is not and should not be confined to *only* gathering evidence for fields because that's all the NGSS asks. This is an idea we'll explore in greater depth in later chapters.

Once you've defined a learning progression, you can start developing individual lessons/activities to use in the classroom, like those in the examples from Figure 3.2. For this, you will take the approach detailed in Chapter 2. Specifically, you'll use the checklist for practice-centric activities to create lessons that build on previously learned material. In Chapters 4–6, I'll demonstrate how my group designed and deployed some example activities within a learning progression like the one shown in Table 3.4.

Creating Assessment Rubrics From Evidence Statements

We have a learning progression and specific practice-based activities. To complete the learning experience, we have to assess the student and our own teaching. As we've discussed, practices are thoughtful actions, as opposed to learned content, so our approach to assessing practices can and should be different from our traditional approach to assessing content knowledge alone. Standardized tests typically focus on the student's proficiency in recalling learned facts and can be a fairly efficient way of measuring learned content knowledge. However, how effective would a similar assessment be at measuring practices?

It actually goes deeper than just assessing practices, though, due to the tight integration between practice and content found in the NGSS. In the last chapter, we discussed situated cognition as an action-based model for how students learn. Students can only "understand" science ideas if they understand how the practice of science leads to those ideas. With respect to content, that means that we should not only assess the student's practice abilities, but we should assess content knowledge within the context of practice, too.

Well-developed multiple-choice tests can be great for measuring content knowledge. However, practices are actions, and the types of activities students do when practicing science are multi-faceted and open-ended. This makes assessment design for practices more difficult. Scoring rubrics, however, can provide the flexibility such activity requires, while also maintaining a structure on which students can base learning. Rubric design experts Dannielle Stevens and Antonia Levi (2005, p. 3) describe the scoring rubric as follows:

> At its most basic, a rubric is a scoring tool that lays out the specific expectations for an assignment. Rubrics divide an assignment into its component parts and provide a detailed description of what constitutes acceptable or unacceptable levels of performance for each of those parts.

There are entire books and websites on designing good rubrics. In particular, I refer you to the University of Colorado Denver's excellent online rubric writing tutorial or Stevens's and Levi's book, both of which are listed in the references (The Center for Faculty Development, University of Colorado Denver, 2006; Stevens & Levi, 2005). Educational consultant Charlotte Danielson has an excellent series of books on rubric design and performance tasks for mathematics published by Routledge Eye on Education that can provide insight to your science lessons (Danielson & Hansen, 2016; Danielson & Dragoon, 2016; Danielson & Marquez, 2016). However, how can we incorporate the generic lessons on rubric design into a system from creating rubrics that assess student work in science practice *and* content all at the same time?

Table 3.5 shows the basic steps to rubric design for integrated practice and content that I will detail here. These steps are based on the research on rubrics and general assessment, specifically tailored to our needs with respect to the NGSS and the *Framework* (Stevens & Levi, 2005). First, we determine the learning goal for the activity. Then, we define the science practice evidence statements to look for in student work. We define

TABLE 3.5 STEPS TO CREATING A RUBRIC THAT ASSESSES SCIENCE PRACTICE IN CONTEXT.

Step	Description
1	Determine the learning goal for the activity.
2	Define the science practice evidence statements to look for in student work.
3	Define individual criterions based on the content.
4	Design a rating scale, with descriptions of expectations for each criterion.
5	Re-evaluate the rubric.

individual criterions based on the content of interest. For each criterion, we design a rating scale and write descriptions of expectations for each criterion. Finally, we deploy the rubric and re-evaluate everything based on student feedback and results.

We have already discussed the first step, determining the learning goal. For the second step, each of the performance expectations laid out in the NGSS comes with an associated set of *evidence statements*. Evidence statements describe what you can look for in student work to provide evidence of understanding. These evidence statements are very useful, since they can serve as the foundation for our assessment rubrics. Table 3.6 shows the basic evidence statements you would look for with respect to the example performance expectation we've been using:

MS-PS2–5. Conduct an investigation and evaluate the experimental design to provide evidence that fields exist between objects exerting forces on each other even though the objects are not in contact.

When assessing a student's work conducting an investigation and evaluating the experimental design, we're looking for five pieces of evidence:

The student

1. Identifies the phenomenon being investigated
2. Identifies the purpose of the investigation
3. Plans the investigation
4. Collects and records the data
5. Evaluates the design

TABLE 3.6 EVIDENCE STATEMENTS FOR CONDUCTING AN INVESTIGATION AND EVALUATING DESIGN. ADAPTED FROM NGSS LEAD STATES (2013B).

	The student
1	Identifies the phenomenon to be investigated
2	Identifies evidence to address the purpose of the investigation
3	Plans the investigation
4	Collects the data
5	Evaluates the design

These evidence statements are general for all of the performance expectations dealing with the science practice of conducting investigations. The specific context will change with varying DCIs. Evidence statements for all of the performance expectations can be found on the website for the NGSS (nextgenscience.org) and can serve as the foundation for assessment rubrics that you can use both for formative and summative assessment (NGSS Lead States, 2013b).

Example 3.1 shows a partial rubric based on the NGSS evidence statements for an activity completed based on performance expectation **MS-PS2–5**. The overall layout of the rubric at the top level is generic across all activities where the student would conduct and evaluate an investigation. At the lower level, the rubric is specific for the individual activity or activities, in this case, for an investigation that produces evidence of fields.

Example 3.1 Partial rubric for conducting and evaluating an investigation on magnetic fields

Identifies the phenomenon to be investigated			
	Unsatisfactory	**Needs Improvement**	**Satisfactory**
Identifies the phenomenon under investigation	The student makes no attempt to identify the phenomenon.	The student identifies the phenomenon, but it is the incorrect phenomenon or is unclear.	The student clearly identifies the correct phenomenon based on the plan.
Identifies the purpose of the investigation	The student makes no attempt to identify the purpose of the investigation.	The student makes an attempt to identify the purpose, but it is unclear.	The student clearly identifies the purpose of the investigation.
Identifies evidence to address the purpose of the investigation			
	Unsatisfactory	**Needs Improvement**	**Satisfactory**
Identifies evidence that two interacting objects can exert forces on each other even though the two interacting objects are not in contact	The student does not identify evidence.	The student makes an attempt to identify the evidence, but it is unclear.	The student identifies the evidence.

(Continued)

Example 3.1 (Continued)

Identifies evidence that the cause of a force on one object is the interaction with the other object	The student does not identify evidence.	The student makes an attempt to identify the evidence, but it is unclear.	The student identifies the evidence.
Plans the investigation			
	Unsatisfactory	**Needs Improvement**	**Satisfactory**
Describes how the magnetic field will be measured with the available equipment	The student does not describe how the magnetic field will be measured.	The student describes how the magnetic field will be measured, but the measurement either can't be done with the materials provided, or will not result in measuring the magnetic field.	The student describes how the magnetic field will be measured, and it will result in a useful measurement.
The plan takes into account changes in distance between objects.	The plan does not take into account.	The plan takes into account, but it is unclear.	The plan does take into account.
The plan takes into account changing magnetic orientations.	The plan does not take into account.	The plan takes into account, but it is unclear.	The plan does take into account.
The plan takes into account varying strength of the magnetic force.	The plan does not take into account.	The plan takes into account, but it is unclear.	The plan does take into account.

Let's look at how I went through the entire hybrid curriculum development process (Figure 3.1) to arrive at the rubric in Example 3.1. I first identified the learning goal and then decided on a learning progression, as detailed in the previous section (Step 1 in Table 3.5). Then, I built individual activities in the learning progression, one of which might directly address the specific performance expectation. I used the evidence statements provided by the NGSS to design the top level of the rubric (Step 2).

The individual criteria below the top level are based on the particular activity and what specific content goals I hope to achieve with the students through the activity or activities (Step 3). Notice that the more generic top-level categories outline the science practice of interest, whereas the individual criterions focus on how the specific content is integrated into practice. Rubrics designed based on this model and the evidence statements naturally integrate the assessment of practice *and* content, as is expected under the NGSS.

Next, we define the rating scale (Step 4). Notice that for each evidence statement and sub-criterion in Example 3.1, the student can achieve a score of either unsatisfactory, needs improvement, or satisfactory. This is where the final re-evaluation step (Step 5) will be necessary to hone your rubric with time and experience. It is usually fairly easy to know what we *want* from the student. It is more difficult to anticipate what the student will actually do. That makes successful rubric building an iterative process, since there are many available paths to the student. As you begin to assess students, you will start to see what little aspects they need to improve on their way towards the goal. This will allow you to do two things: (1) design better, more detailed rubrics for future use, and (2) make changes to the learning experience that can lead to the improvement you seek. Again, that's the evaluative step in curriculum development that's key if you want to involve students and their feedback into the learning process (and also Step 5 in rubric writing).

You should think of the rubric as a guide *for the student*, as opposed to merely an assessment instrument. In fact, as we'll discuss later in this chapter, you will want to give your students any rubric you will use to assess an assignment *before* they are tasked with the assignment, including tests. This makes your descriptions of expectations a key learning tool for the student, serving as a learning guide they can use during their performance. The clearer your descriptions of your expectations are, the easier it will be for the student to meet those expectations. Also, it's critically important that the same types of rubrics used for low-stakes formative assessment are also used when the time comes to test students. It is unfair of you to move the target!

Think-Pair-Share: Formative Assessment in the Moment

Formative assessment in the moment is also an important and immediately available source of feedback we can use in our teaching. Assignment rubrics are great for assessing students after the activity. However, it's even better when we can assess the student in the moment. That is to say, we can determine what the student can and cannot do and what they have and have not learned while they are participating in the activity. This provides immediate feedback that can be used for intervention in-the-moment, before bad habits become ingrained. The in-the-moment assessment/learning technique called "think-pair-share" or "peer instruction" is perfect for this (Lyman, 1987; Mazur, 1997).

Think-pair-share is not specifically an assessment technique, but more a cooperative learning technique that encourages individual participation in a student-led, community discussion. We're going to discuss how to use it not only as a learning opportunity and community-building activity, but also as an in-the-moment assessment.

Think-pair-share is a three-step process deployed before, after, or in the middle of an activity:

1. *Think:* A question is posed by the teacher, and students independently form their own ideas. When questions are posed in a multiple-choice format, the students can then be polled, providing the teacher immediate feedback on student learning.
2. *Pair:* After individual thinking, students form pairs or small groups to discuss their thoughts and what they believe to be the correct answer. Notice that this forces the students to articulate their thoughts and to consider the thoughts of others. Ideally, the group forms a consensus, with clearer ideas prevailing.
3. *Share:* The students then share their ideas with the larger class, where all ideas can be discussed.

Notice that in this short 3-step process, we're actually achieving quite a lot. First, we're making the student individually responsible for his or her own thinking. When we poll students, we as teachers get to see their individual responses before having time to discuss with the group. This allows us to determine which students are quickly grasping material and which are not. It also prevents students from "getting by" through the efforts of others in their group, while performance on independent assignments, like tests, suffer without the teacher ever knowing why.

Second, we are forcing reflection, which we've already discussed the importance of in Chapter 2's mantra: "Be explicit. Be reflective. Make it count." When grouped up, there is no "authority" or "expert" with the "correct" idea. It's just other students. Therefore, ideas must win or lose based on the power of the argument and evidence presented. It's easy for a student to simply accept what the teacher says with little thought. To accept what their peer says requires persuasion on the part of the peer and reflection on their own thinking. This results in students taking ownership of their learning, with meaning being negotiated in a community rather than based on the teacher's authority (Cobb et al., 1991). Because the students are participating in a negotiation, rather than memorizing facts, their views about science can also begin to shift.

So, how would we implement think-pair-share in a practice-centric activity? Example 3.2 shows two multiple-choice questions we could use in class during a learning progression on magnetism. Both questions probe the student's ability to recognize the elements necessary in an experiment that tests a specific hypothesis. To correctly answer each question, the student must have developed both specific content knowledge in magnetism *and* the ability to plan an investigation.

Example 3.2 Think-pair-share questions for conducting investigations on magnetism

1. A student has observed that paperclips become magnetized after they are in contact with a magnet. The student hypothesizes the following:

   "A magnet consists of smaller pieces of magnet that are transferred via contact from the magnet to the paperclip."

   Which of the following proposes a testing experiment for this hypothesis?

   A. Observe if the paperclip becomes magnetized.
   B. Hold the paperclip to the opposite pole and observe whether or not the paperclip becomes magnetized.
   C. Get a different magnet and a different paperclip and observe whether or not the paperclip becomes magnetized after being in contact with the new magnet.
   D. Hold the same paperclip away from the same magnet and observe if it remains magnetized.

   (Continued)

Example 3.2 (Continued)

    E. Get a new paperclip that is initially un-magnetized and hold it near the magnet without touching. Observe whether the new paperclip becomes magnetized.

2. When the continents on Earth were first forming, the land was very hot and molten and contained many ferromagnetic materials. The Earth then cooled as the continents were formed. It is proposed that the continents are not in the same locations around the Earth today as they were when they first cooled. Four students are discussing how it could be determined whether or not this proposal is accurate:

    Student A: We could use a compass to determine in which direction is the Earth's magnetic north pole. If it's different than the pole on which the Earth spins, then we know the continents have moved.

    Student B: I think we should conduct a controlled experiment, where we hold all independent variables constant. Then we can measure the movement of the continents.

    Student C: The continents have moved, so we should see where they are now and piece them back together like a puzzle to determine how they fit a long time ago before they moved.

    Student D: The magnetic orientation of the ferromagnetic material deep in the ground could give us clues as to how the continents were oriented a long time ago. If they don't line up with each other around the globe, then we have evidence that the continents have moved.

Which student has the best approach to coming up with experimental evidence that could support the proposition?

Before beginning an activity where the student plans an investigation, I pose one of these questions to the entire class. First, students think about the question as individuals. Then, I poll the class to get instant feedback on each student's thinking. I use sheets of paper with large letters A, B, C, and D printed on them that can be folded to display their choice. After students register their answer, I immediately know both the percentage of students that have the correct answer, and where those students are sitting in the classroom. I can then pair students up for a discussion based on their responses. Usually, I say the following: "Find someone that you disagree with and convince them that you are right and they are wrong." After discussion, I can re-poll the class.

This short activity serves several purposes: It provides immediate low-stakes formative assessment on student thinking with respect to practice and content, and it prepares the student for the coming activity. Furthermore, it signals to the student what will be made to count in the classroom: science practice. For further assessment, we can use similar questions on pencil-and-paper examinations, either in the same multiple-choice format or open-ended.

Summative Assessment of Science Practice

Eventually, we must raise the stakes and administer tests that summatively assess each student's individual abilities. Your summative assessments should look similar to your formative assessments. With this in mind, we can look back at how we formatively assessed science practice in context, and use these same principles to summatively assess the individual. We ultimately have three options: (1) pencil-and-paper tests, (2) activity-based tests, and/or (3) a combination of both.

As discussed above, questions similar to those we used in the think-pair-share activities can be used as test questions in pencil-and-paper tests. For example, the questions shown in Example 3.2 could be used as test questions in either the multiple-choice format shown, or in an open-ended format. We could also look at the individual components of the evidence statements to create new questions that probe students on a part-by-part basis.

The other option for testing practice is to actually have the student engage in practice. It makes sense that if students learn by doing science, and we teach by having them do science, then we should assess them while they are actually doing science. These types of assessments are what I call "activity-based tests." They are ultimately mini-projects that the student completes individually.

Example 3.3 shows an example of an activity-based test and the corresponding rubric that would be used to score the test. In this particular test, we have the students plan and conduct an investigation on the effect stacking magnets has on the magnitude of the force. Students are provided a very limited set of materials that they are allowed to use in their investigation. The rubric is attached and provided to the student before the test. Furthermore, the rubric has the same structure as the rubrics used during the regular class time. Therefore, the expectations are not only clear, but the student should have had the opportunity to practice meeting those same expectations in different contexts. I actually give my students the test the day before they will have to complete it in class, to provide enough time for thinking and planning.

Example 3.3 Summative assessment for conducting an investigation on magnetic strength

In this activity, you will individually plan and conduct an experiment that determines how the strength of the magnetic force depends on the number of magnets stacked in a stable configuration. You will be provided with five unmarked, circular magnets, several paperclips, and a ruler. You may use only these items to conduct the experiment. All work must be recorded in your scientific notebook.

Your work will be graded based on the following rubric:

Identifies the phenomenon to be investigated			
	Unsatisfactory	Needs Improvement	Satisfactory
Identifies the phenomenon under investigation	The student makes no attempt to identify the phenomenon.	The student identifies the phenomenon, but it is the incorrect phenomenon or is unclear.	The student clearly identifies the correct phenomenon based on the plan.
Identifies the purpose of the investigation	The student makes no attempt to identify the purpose of the investigation.	The student makes an attempt to identify the purpose, but it is unclear.	The student clearly identifies the purpose of the investigation.

(Continued)

Example 3.3 (Continued)

Identifies evidence to address the purpose of the investigation			
	Unsatisfactory	**Needs Improvement**	**Satisfactory**
Develops an investigation plan that describes the data to be collected	The student makes no attempt to describe the data to be collected.	The student makes an attempt to describe the data to be collected, but it is unclear or does not distinguish the variables.	The student describes the data that will be collected, including independent and dependent variables.
Develops an investigation plan that describes the evidence to be derived from the data	The student makes no attempt to describe the evidence to be derived from the data.	The student makes an attempt to describe that evidence, but it is unclear or the proposed evidence cannot answer the research question.	The student described the evidence to be derived from the data, including how the data will be used to answer the research question.
Plans the investigation			
	Unsatisfactory	**Needs Improvement**	**Satisfactory**
Describes how the magnetic force will be measured with the available equipment	The student does not describe how the magnetic force will be measured.	The student describes how the magnetic force will be measured, but the measurement either can't be done with the materials provided, or will not result in measuring the magnetic force.	The student describes how the magnetic force will be measured, and it will result in a useful measurement.
Collects the data			
	Unsatisfactory	**Needs Improvement**	**Satisfactory**
Makes and records observations according to the given plan	No observations are recorded.	Observations are recorded, but not based on the given plan OR observations are incorrectly recorded OR the record is unclear.	Observations are recorded clearly and in accordance with the given plan.
Makes a graph that shows how the magnetic force depends on the number of magnets	No graph is provided.	A graph is provided, but does not display the collected data OR is improperly labeled OR is not labeled at all.	A graph is provided that properly displays the collected data AND is correctly labeled.

Figure 3.3 shows an example of student work on the activity-based test shown in Example 3.3. In this sample of student work, we see the student's recorded data and can get an idea of how they decided to measure the magnetic force. This student used the ruler to measure how far away the paperclip needed to rest before being attracted to the face of the magnet. The force measurement is being made in units of fractions of inches. The student can then plot the force as a function of the number of magnets (not shown).

You will actually be amazed at how readily students come up with ingenious ways to make measurements with limited amounts of materials. The natural tendency is to reach for a "magnetic force meter," but no such device really exists. You'll also be amazed at how much students enjoy being tested in this manner. It's not *really* a test. They're playing!

There are several keys to good activity-based tests. First, they should be relatively short and simple activities. The materials also need to be small and plentiful. In our case, it is easy for a student to work as an individual at their

Figure 3.3 Example recorded data from a student exam on conducting an investigation to determine the effect of stacking magnets on the magnetic strength.

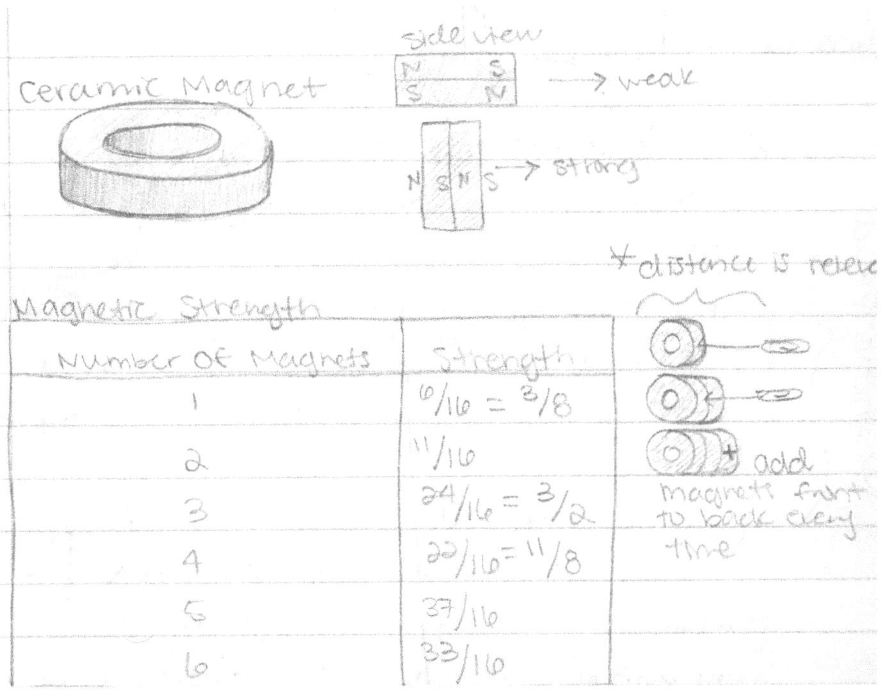

desk using a few small magnets, paperclips, and a ruler. However, if we instead attempted to have them roll bowling balls down the hall and measure speed, then that would be impractical for any normal-size class. It might make an excellent group activity, but a terrible activity-based test.

Summary

In summary, we've looked at developing curriculum with the assessment of science practice in context on our minds. Specifically, we discussed a hybrid product/process framework for curriculum development that provides a solid foundation for developing learning goals and experiences, but allows the flexibility to adjust based on student feedback. We discussed how to use the NGSS performance expectations to set realizable learning goals, and how to build a learning progression that scaffolds instruction toward those goals. The corresponding NGSS evidence statements were used to design assessment rubrics, multiple-choice, and open-ended questions for both formative and summative assessment. And finally, we discussed how to make final tests action based to better align with our goal of teaching and assessing the action of science.

The following is a brief summary of the main points:

- Assessment must be built into curriculum design. You can't have one without the other.
- Curriculum is best thought of as a process, as opposed to a series of products.
- NGSS performance expectations can be used to define learning goals.
- In designing a learning progression that achieves our learning goals, we must go beyond the NGSS. Just because content isn't in the NGSS, or because a certain practice isn't used with some specific content, doesn't mean we can't use it in our classes. Sometimes we must!
- NGSS evidence statements provide a useful foundation for writing assessments.
- Good rubrics are consistent in their top-level approach with respect to practices, with individual criterion requiring specific content knowledge. Therefore, good rubrics combine the assessment of science practice and science content *at the same time*.

- Think-pair-share is a phenomenal activity in and of itself, but also serves as a terrific opportunity for individual formative assessment *in-the-moment*.
- If we're going to have students do science during class time, then we should do our best to test them in the same way: by having them do science. Activity-based tests allow for the assessment of practices and content, while having the added benefit of being fun.

References

The Center for Faculty Development, University of Colorado Denver. (2006). *Creating a Rubric: An Online Tutorial for Faculty*. Retrieved from www.ucdenver.edu/faculty_staff/faculty/center-for-faculty-development/Documents/Tutorials/Rubrics/index.htm

Cobb, P., Wood, T., Yackel, E., Nicholls, J., Wheatley, G., Trigatti, B., and Perlwitz, M. (1991). Assessment of a problem-centered second-grade mathematics project. *Journal for Research in Mathematics Education*, 22(1), 3–29.

Cornbleth, C. (1990). *Curriculum in Context*. Basingstoke: Falmer Press.

Danielson, C., & Dragoon, J. (2016). *Performance Tasks and Rubrics for Upper Elementary Mathematics* (2nd ed.). New York: Routledge.

Danielson, C., & Hansen, P. (2016). *Performance Tasks and Rubrics for Early Elementary Mathematics* (2nd ed.). New York: Routledge.

Danielson, C., & Marquez, E. (2016). *Performance Tasks and Rubrics for Middle School Mathematics* (2nd ed.). New York: Routledge.

Grundy, S. (1987). *Curriculum: Product or Praxis?* New York, NY: Falmer Press.

Lyman, F. (1987). Think-pair-share: An ending teaching technique. *MAA-CIE Cooperative News*, 1, 1–2.

Mazur, E. (1997). *Peer Instruction: A User's Manual Series in Educational Innovation*. Upper Saddle River, NJ: Prentice Hall.

NGSS Lead States. (2013a). APPENDIX E—Progressions Within the Next Generation Science Standards. In N. L. States (Ed.), *Next Generation Science Standards: For States, by States*. Washington, DC: The National Academies Press.

NGSS Lead States. (2013b). *Evidence Statements*. Retrieved from Next Generation Science Standards: www.nextgenscience.org

NGSS Lead States. (2013c). *Next Generation Science Standards: For States, by States*. Washington, DC: The National Academies Press.

Smith, M. K. (2000). *Curriculum Theory and Practice*. Retrieved from The Encyclopedia of Informal Education: www.infed.org/biblio/b-curric.htm

Stenhouse, L. (1975). *An Introduction to Curriculum Research and Development*. London: Heinemann.

Stevens, D. D., & Levi, A. J. (2005). *An Introduction to Rubrics*. Sterling, VA: Stylus.

Stiggins, R., & Chappuis, J. (2017). *Introduction to Student-Involved Assessment FOR Learning* (7th ed.). New York, NY: Pearson.

Taba, H. (1962). *Curriculum Development: Theory and Practice*. New York, NY: Harcourt Brace and World.

Tyler, R. W. (1949). *Basic Principles of Curriculum and Instruction*. Chicago: University of Chicago Press.

Wragg, T. (1997). *The Cubic Curriculum*. London: Routledge.

Part II
Science Practice in the Classroom

4

Conducting Investigations and Transforming Your Classroom

"Crucial to science education is hands-on involvement: showing, not just telling; real experiments and field trips and not just 'virtual reality.'"
—Martin Rees (2011)

The foundation of science is the investigation. Scientists learn about how the world behaves by asking good questions, observing and recognizing patterns, developing and using models of physical behavior, and conducting experiments that can test those models. Investigations are also fun! The science practice dimension of investigation revolves around doing experiments, which for many young children is functionally equivalent to playing. Like we discussed in Chapter 2, cognitive apprenticeship as a teaching theory requires us to get the student involved in the authentic practice of science. Therefore, the first step toward transforming your classroom instruction to better align with the Next Generation Science Standards (NGSS) is to begin focusing learning and teaching around the practice of investigation. Doing so will also make your class more fun for the student and promote learning of practice at the same time.

We've discussed the theory on classroom reform in Chapter 2. But, what does a classroom based around cognitive apprenticeship look like in practice? How can you take what you currently do in the classroom and modify it to include science practices? In this chapter, we'll look at some simple examples of teaching through investigations. Specifically, I'll show you real-world examples from the teaching and learning of light reflection. First, I will show you an example of traditional content-focused instruction pulled from a real fourth-grade classroom, and how that same content can easily be taught in a manner that aligns with the NGSS. Specifically, I'll show you a learning progression you can go through to teach students about light, the ray model, and how to design experiments that answer questions about light reflection. I'll use the checklist for activity development from Chapter 2 as a guide, I'll take advantage of the framework for developing assessable curriculum discussed in Chapter 3, and I'll demonstrate real student work and how it was assessed.

It's important to realize that this is not intended as a chapter about teaching light reflection specifically, but a chapter about teaching the practices of investigation within some context. I don't want you to focus too much on the content. I want you to think about how the content and activities are being used to teach the practices. Even though your specific content may differ, the approach to teaching through practice will be the same. Specifically, in this chapter you'll learn about teaching the distinction between scientific and non-scientific questions. We'll examine how to design lessons that have students creating useful mental models for content pulled from their own experiences. I'll describe how to teach pattern recognition, and how students can use that to create useful physical models that they can use to make predictions. Finally, we'll look at the types of experiments scientists design and execute, and more importantly, how to get students to the point where they can come up with their own experiments. All of these activities are necessary to the practicing scientist, whether the context is light reflection or seed dispersion and plant pollination. Don't let the specific physical science example fool you into thinking that this stuff is only applicable to physical science!

Moving Away From Sage-on-the-Stage and Towards Discovery

Let's start by looking at a modern version of what could be called "traditional" content-focused instruction. Figure 4.1 shows a picture of one page from a science notebook collected from a fourth-grade science class in South Carolina. In this particular example, the content is the reflection of

Figure 4.1 An actual example from a fourth-grade student's science notebook.

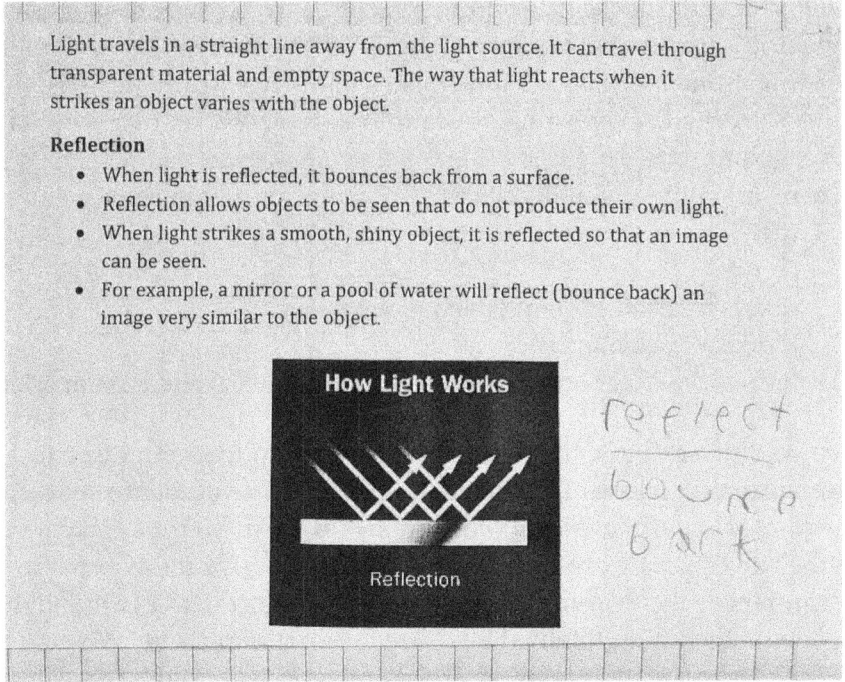

light. Each day in this classroom, students would be provided printed content that they would be expected to paste into the notebook. The teacher then leads a discussion of the content, working with the student to highlight certain information. For some material, a demonstration might be performed, or there may be some sort of short activity. However, these demonstrations and activities never make it into the notebook. Sometimes, the student takes "notes" in the margin of their notebook. In Figure 4.1, we see the student writing "reflection = bounce back," as an indication of the main point of the presented material. Students are instructed to read through recent entries in their scientific notebooks each evening in preparation for exams on the content.

What we are looking at here is a modern-day manifestation of the "sage-on-the-stage" model of instruction. An expert stands at the front of the class and tells the student what is important to know. The student absorbs this information and then repeats it back to the expert on some formal exam sometime in the future, thereby demonstrating that they have learned it. In this particular case, we are merely replacing the textbook constructed by a publisher with one physically constructed by the student, although there is functionally no difference between the student reading either. Furthermore, there is just as little focus on practices and abilities as reading from a textbook, unless the ability we want the student to acquire happens to be pasting pages into a notebook and creating tables of content and indices. *The student is not doing science.*

There are fundamentally three problems with this read-memorize-repeat approach to science education. They are as follows:

1. It fails to teach content effectively.
2. It doesn't teach practices at all.
3. It does the exact opposite of getting students excited about science.

As we've discussed in Chapter 2, this approach to teaching reinforces the novice view that science is a collection of facts. The student sees a series of terms that may or may not correspond to their everyday experiences with the subject. They are told to essentially memorize these terms so that they can repeat them in the future. Important information is highlighted. (What about the un-highlighted bits? Are they not important? Why are they there?) The student that is good at this memorization and possesses the patience to study will perform well at this task. However, do they *understand* light reflection? Is that student prepared for assessment based on the NGSS? Could they develop and use a model for light after this exercise?

On the subject of models, I want you to think about the image of light reflection shown in Figure 4.1. This representation of light bouncing off a surface is a very specific mental model for light called the *ray model of light*. For fourth graders, this would be their very first exposure to a ray model of light. Imagine what is happening in the students' mind when they first see this representation, and consider the students' real-world experience with light. Does light actually physically look like this? Do we see individual little beams bouncing off surfaces in the real world? No. The image represents a mental model for light that can be used to make predictions about how light will behave, but it does not represent the actual physical reality.

Often times, as is done in this example, we provide these mental models without further explanation, leaving their purpose and significance implied instead of explicitly stated. This further serves to separate the student from expert-like views of science. To students, science is the learning of facts that often don't have significance to the real world around them. How will these little light arrows serve the student? What information does the representation provide to help the student understand? Other than "reflection = bounce back," not much.

I want you to think about the presentation of content shown in Figure 4.1 from the perspective of the highly inquisitive student with attention issues, or the bright student whose first language isn't English? Would this style of instruction be effective for these students? In their minds, they see a "word salad" combined with an image that makes no sense. We discussed this in more detail in Chapter 2, but there is decades of consistent research demonstrating that teaching content by telling is only moderately effective in the sciences for some students, and absolutely fails for students considered even moderately at risk (Hake, 1998; Lord & Orkwiszewski, 2006). Pasting material into a notebook is an example of attempting to actively engage students in their learning, but not in the right ways. The concept of a scientific notebook itself is excellent, as we'll discuss in more detail throughout the book; however, this particular execution misses the central point of scientific documentation: We document experiences.

So what can we do differently? That is what this chapter is about. I want you to start thinking about the content and its presentation from the viewpoint of the student and not your own "weird" viewpoint. I also want you to start thinking about teaching content such as reflection through the practices we discussed in Chapter 1. We're going to use the research and the checklist discussed in Chapter 2 to develop activities that teach practices in the context of the same content from Figure 4.1. How might this simple material be transformed into a practice-centric learning experience based on cognitive apprenticeship?

Reflection of Light Through Science Practice

Instead of the content focus seen in the previous section, we're going to learn how to focus instruction on the investigation dimension of the science practices. As a reminder, Table 4.1 details the science practices outlined by the *Framework* that I have grouped into the investigation dimension (National Research Council, 2012). The investigation dimension consists of the following practices:

1. Asking questions
2. Developing and using models
3. Planning and carrying out investigations

TABLE 4.1 SCIENCE PRACTICES WITHIN THE DIMENSION OF INVESTIGATIONS.

Science Practice	Description
Asking questions	Science begins by asking questions. In particular, the student must learn the distinction between a scientific question and an un-scientific question. The distinction centers on whether the question can or cannot be answered through empirical evidence, either collected by the student, or someone else.
Developing and using models	Models are representations of the physical world that allow the scientist to predict future behavior. Models are typically approximations of the real world, and typically consist of diagrams, an analogy, a mathematical equation, and/or a simulation on the computer. The student must learn how to develop models through observations, and how to use models to make predictions.
Planning and conducting investigations	Investigations can be as simple as formal observation of the world around the scientist, up to systematic studies across multiple variables. The sophistication of the investigations should increase as the student progresses through the grade levels. The student must learn to make observations, plan and conduct experiments that test hypotheses, and implement investigations that can solve problems.

We're going to look at how you can teach the same content on light reflection through the practice of investigation. Specifically, we'll look at what an apprenticeship-based fourth-grade lesson for light reflection would look like, where the content is taught through these three science practices.

Table 4.2 details the content from Figure 4.1 and the corresponding NGSS-based student performance expectations we will use in our activity development (NGSS Lead States, 2013b). Ultimately, we want to teach the student about the following content:

1. How light reflects off varying surfaces
2. How light reflects off mirrors
3. The ray model of light as a means to make predictions

This represents our learning progression and will be accomplished by leading the students through science practice activities that have them asking questions, developing and using models, and planning and conducting investigations.

In Table 4.2, performance expectations in bold come directly from the NGSS. For each content area, I also show a new performance expectation that is not explicitly listed in the NGSS. I discussed this in Chapter 1 and

TABLE 4.2 AN EXAMPLE ELEMENTARY-LEVEL LEARNING PROGRESSION FOR THE REFLECTION OF LIGHT. BOLDED LABELS REPRESENT PERFORMANCE EXPECTATIONS TAKEN DIRECTLY FROM THE NGSS (NGSS LEAD STATES, 2013A).

Content	NGSS-Based Performance Expectation
Light reflection	Students who demonstrate understanding can ♦ *Ask questions* about the behavior of light ♦ (**1-PS4–2**) *Make observations* to construct an evidence-based account that objects in darkness can be seen only when illuminated
Reflection off mirrors	Students who demonstrate understanding can ♦ (**4-PS4–2**) *Develop a model* to describe that light reflecting from objects and entering the eye allows objects to be seen
The ray model of light	Students who demonstrate understanding can ♦ *Develop and use a model* for reflection to predict how light will behave when reflected off a mirror ♦ *Design and conduct an investigation* that tests the hypothesis that rays of light reflect off mirrors at the same angle in which they hit the mirror

Chapter 3, but it bears repeating: The NGSS is a *minimum* set of standards and not curriculum. It's perfectly acceptable and even necessary to expand on both the content and practices described in the NGSS, especially if it helps strengthen student understanding about a topic. Basically, to have students develop a model as required by **4-PS4–2**, we're also going to need them to ask questions and design and conduct investigations, too, even though those particular practices aren't tied to a specific NGSS performance expectation for light. This is an idea we'll explore in greater depth in Chapter 7.

Light and its reflection from surfaces is covered under the NGSS in the first and fourth grades, as seen in the performance expectations listed in Table 4.2. This aligns with our fourth-grade science notebook page shown in Figure 4.1. The notebook shown came from a South Carolina classroom. South Carolina has not adopted the NGSS; however, the South Carolina science standards are based on the *Framework* and are therefore similar to the NGSS in Disciplinary Core Ideas (DCIs) and practices, at least with respect to light reflection (South Carolina Department of Education, 2014).

In the first grade, students are expected to understand light reflection by making observations of and planning investigations on how light interacts with various objects. Fundamentally, we want students to recognize through evidence that objects can only be seen when illuminated and that light behaves differently when different objects are placed in its path, such as mirrors, beakers of water, and opaque objects.

In the fourth grade, the student expands on these observations and begins to develop a model that they can use to predict light behavior when reflected off mirrors. Although we will not discuss it in this chapter, the fourth-grade student will also develop and use a more formal model for the refraction of light. As the student moves into middle school, the same material will be learned with increasing sophistication. Specifically, students will begin the discovery of the wave nature of light as a means to explain both reflection and refraction. And finally, in high school, the student will develop a more sophisticated electromagnetic wave model and photon model of light, with more sophisticated mathematical modeling of light behavior.

Again, we see two key features of the NGSS: (1) content progresses and (2) practices are consistent across age groups. Throughout the progression in learning about light, students are consistently exposed to the same practices of science over and over again, even as the execution of those practices and the content gets more and more sophisticated. In the following sections, we will go through the learning progression for light and its reflection from first to fourth grade. These are merely examples to help you learn how to create your own lessons, whether you teach elementary school, middle school, or high school science. Because of the cross-cutting nature of practice, even the high school biology teacher should find these examples illuminating.

I also want you to understand how I know the learning progression for light and how you can easily determine the NGSS learning progression for the content you need to teach. Listed in the References section at the end of this chapter, Appendix E of the NGSS very clearly lays out the progression for DCIs as they span grade levels (NGSS Lead States, 2013a). For the example of light, the relevant DCI is *PS4.B Electromagnetic Radiation*, with the progression summarized here in Table 4.3. Before beginning the development of any NGSS activities, you should first refer to the progression for the content listed in Appendix E, since it is critical that you know to what a student should have already been exposed, and what they will be expected to do in the future. As we will see, content builds and good teaching draws on the student's past experiences.

TABLE 4.3 DCI GRADE-LEVEL PROGRESSION FOR ELECTROMAGNETIC RADIATION (LIGHT) SUMMARIZED FROM THE NGSS APPENDIX E: PROGRESSIONS WITHIN THE NEXT GENERATION SCIENCE STANDARDS (NGSS LEAD STATES, 2013A).

Grade Level	Progression
K–2	Objects can be seen only when light is available to illuminate them.
3–5	Objects can be seen when light reflected from their surface enters our eyes.
6–8	The construct of a wave is used to model how light interacts with objects.
9–12	Both an electromagnetic wave model and a photon model explain features of electromagnetic radiation broadly and describe common applications of electromagnetic radiation.

Asking Scientific Questions

Let's start with basic light reflection and the practice of asking questions. Science begins by asking good questions and being curious about the world around us. In particular, the student of science must learn the distinction between a scientific question and a non-scientific question. The distinction centers on whether the question can or cannot be answered through empirical evidence, either collected by the student, or someone else. In this first example, how can we teach students the practice of asking scientific questions about light? How can we teach the content we want them to know through the lens of practice?

First, let's look at the performance expectation.

Students who demonstrate understanding can
- *Ask questions* about the behavior of light

Once you have decided that this is what you want your students to be able to do, you now have to design a short lesson that will have students ask questions that lead to greater understanding of light. This is where we will use the research and the checklist from Chapter 2 as a guide. In particular, *situated cognition* tells us that learning happens through doing, and *cognitive apprenticeship* tells us to teach by having the learner do. In this specific case, we need to ultimately get students to start asking scientific questions on their own.

Table 4.4 shows the checklist for an effective apprenticeship activity for this performance expectation. Using this checklist, we have set-up the

TABLE 4.4 SAMPLE CHECKLIST FOR AN APPRENTICESHIP-BASED ACTIVITY APPLIED TO THE PRACTICE OF ASKING QUESTIONS ABOUT THE BEHAVIOR OF LIGHT.

Checklist	Description
Identify the practice and content	A student that demonstrates understanding can *ask questions* about the behavior of light. Specifically, we want students to think about what happens when lights are turned on, and how this affects how we see objects.
Identify how the student will construct knowledge	For the first or fourth grader, we will model how to ask scientific questions, and then coach them toward asking their own questions. We'll start by asking the questions: What would happen if there was no light? What would we see? Then, we will coach students toward asking the question: How can we see objects that don't make their own light?
Define the community the student will work within	We will start off modeling the first scientific question and having students talk with each other in small groups about what they think. Then, the class will meet for a whole-class conference where their group's ideas are shared.
Define the explicit instruction to be given	We will be explicit about the practice of asking scientific questions. We will be explicit in describing the difference between scientific and non-scientific questions.
Identify how you will encourage reflection	We want students to reflect on the difference between a scientific and non-scientific question. We will use two think-pair-share questions to get students to reflect in their own minds, and then to discuss with their friends.
Define how the activity will be made to count	The think-pair-share questions on asking questions will serve as models for future summative exam questions. We are also signaling to the student that practice matters through our focus on the practice of asking questions, with light behavior being merely our context.

framework for a short activity based on modeling and coaching that develops the student's ability to ask scientific questions and learn about the behavior of light and its interactions with objects. This activity requires no materials or printed pages, since it revolves completely around discussion. This activity could be used in both the first- and the fourth-grade classroom, with slightly different implementations based on the relative differences in reading and writing abilities across these groups. For the fourth-grade classroom and beyond, we would ultimately want to work with the student on documenting the experience, which we will discuss in more detail in Chapter 6. For now, though, we'll only focus on classroom discussion on how to ask scientific questions.

The first item on the checklist is identifying both the practice and the content. In Table 4.4, I have formatted this within the structure of the NGSS performance expectations: A student that demonstrates understanding can ask questions about the behavior of light. Specifically, during this activity, we want students to think about what happens when lights are turned on, and how this affects how we see objects.

Next, we get more specific about what exactly the student (and teacher) will do. What is the actual activity? In this area of the checklist, we want to frame the activity within the cognitive apprenticeship foundation of modeling, coaching, and scaffolding. For this particular activity, we will start off by modeling how to ask scientific questions, and then coach them toward asking their own questions. In the classroom, we'll start by asking the question: What would happen if there was no light? What would we see? Then, we will coach students toward asking the question: How can we see objects that don't make their own light? In class discussions that I have led, I like to introduce a short video showing what a SCUBA diver in a dark cave sees as he or she swims around with a flashlight. There is one point in the video where the diver turns off the flashlight. We also discuss how "new" items in the cave can be seen only when the flashlight is aimed at them.

Note that during the activity, we will need to be explicit about the practice of asking scientific questions. It must be apparent to both the teacher and the student that the focus is on the practice of asking scientific questions, with light being the domain in which those questions are asked. In the classroom, we will be explicit in describing the difference between scientific and non-scientific questions, having students come up with their own versions within the context of light behavior. Forcing students to come up with their own examples of both scientific and non-scientific questions also forces them to reflect on this difference.

At the conclusion of the activity, we will want to use a couple of think-pair-share questions to get students to reflect in their own minds, and then to discuss with their friends. As an example, you could write two questions on the board, with one being an example of a good scientific question, and the other being an example of a non-scientific question. Label these two questions A and B, respectively. Have the students individually determine which they believe to be scientific and display their responses with the letter cards we discussed in Chapter 3. If there are students still struggling making the distinction, then have the students discuss amongst themselves until a consensus is reached.

The think-pair-share questions at the end of the discussion serve as formative assessment that you can use to gauge whether or not students are understanding the practice of asking scientific questions. Also, these think-pair-share questions could serve as models for future summative exam questions. By asking students to use their new experiences with science practice to answer questions, we are also signaling to the student that practices matter. It should be clear to you how the activity makes the practice explicit, has the student reflect, and makes science practice count, as we learned are essential in Chapters 2 and 3.

To summarize, we model the practice of asking scientific and non-scientific questions, and in the process, we are being explicit about the distinction. We coach students toward asking their own scientific questions about light. Students reflect on the difference between scientific and non-scientific questions through discussion with their peers. Finally, we formatively assess students on their ability to distinguish between types of questions through think-pair-share questions, with subsequent discussion resulting in further reflection.

Developing and Using Models

After asking good questions, scientists develop models that can help them understand the world around them. Models are representations of the physical world that allow the scientist to predict future behavior. Models are typically approximations of the real world, and they can consist of diagrams, an analogy, a mathematical equation, and/or a simulation on the computer. The student must learn how to develop models through observations, and how to use models to make predictions.

Here, we will discuss two types of models: the mental model and the physical predictive model. A mental model is a representation of physical reality within the learner's mind that assists with understanding, specifically concepts that have no obviously visible exemplars, such as light. (We can't "see" a light ray directly!) A physical predictive model is a more sophisticated formal model that can be used to make predictions.

The representation in Figure 4.1 is based on the ray model of light, which is a type of mental model, and within the framework of *sage-on-the-stage* instruction, is left implicit. You'll notice, too, that the rays in Figure 4.1 reflect off the mirror at the same angle with which they hit the mirror. Built into this representation is also a physical model of light reflection. It predicts how light "rays" will reflect off mirrors.

These models for light may or may not automatically align with the mental model in the student's mind, if they have even formed one. We want to accomplish more through apprenticeship-based instruction.

Specifically, we want students to not only learn about the ray model, but also learn how models are developed and how to use them. Therefore, we are going to look at activities that guide the student toward building a ray mental model from the ground up, where the student is ultimately the creator of the model. After the student has a clear mental model for light, we want them to expand on this model to create a useful, predictive model for the reflection of light. We'll use reflection off plane mirrors to do this, since it represents the simplest case. Basically, students will create and then use the same representation shown in Figure 4.1; however, they will understand not only what the picture represents, but how such representations are created in the first place. They will have learned content *and* practice.

Let's look at the two performance expectations for developing and using models within the context of light and its reflection. One performance expectation comes directly from the NGSS, while the other is an extension of the NGSS. They are as follows.

Students who demonstrate understanding can

- **(4-PS4–2)** *Develop a model* to describe that light reflecting from objects and entering the eye allows objects to be seen.
- *Develop and use a model* for reflection to predict how light will behave when reflected off a mirror.

As you will see, we actually have to get the student to understand the development of a model for reflection *on the way* toward developing and using that model to understand how objects are seen. How do we best teach the development of models? Cognitive apprenticeship has us model, coach, and scaffold instruction in expert-like practices, but we still have to answer two questions: (1) How does a scientist actually develop a predictive model, like for reflection off mirrors and objects, and (2) how would we use good apprenticeship to get students to form a good mental model for content in their own minds? After all, if we want to teach students how to develop and use a model, we need to know how it's done ourselves so we can mimic that process in the classroom.

Constructing a Mental Model

Let's start with the second question: How do we teach mental model building? We start here, because the learner cannot possibly begin making sense of their world until they have first built a mental model for it (Box, 1979). In particular, we want to teach students how to develop a useful mental model of physical phenomena that they can use to understand.

In Seymour Papert's *constructionist learning*, students are guided through activities where they must construct their own mental models of the world around them, using information they already know to "construct" new knowledge (Alesandrini & Larson, 2002). This means rather than teach-by-telling where the model is just provided, we want students to build models of their world based on their own experiences, either past experiences or based on some new observations they make in the classroom. When students construct their own models, they "own" them. This is powerful, because when a student "creates" knowledge and knows it, then we're automatically instilling in that student an expert-like view of science.

So how can we *lead* them to *discover* the ray model of light? Surprisingly, even students in the first grade already have a fairly sophisticated ray model that they use in their minds when thinking about light. I call this model the "Kindergarten Sun Ray Model of Light." Imagine asking your students to draw a picture of the sun. More than likely, most of the students in the class will draw a picture similar to that shown in Figure 4.2, which shows a picture of the sun produced by a fourth grader. (The inclusion of sunglasses and/or a smiley face is typical. Suns are happy!) Interestingly, I get essentially the same pictures (sunglasses and all) whether I'm working with a group of elementary school children, college physics majors, or in-service teachers. The only difference is that with the older groups, there is usually one or two students that draw a *very accurate* picture of the sun, complete with sun spots, flares, and a fairly good depiction of the corona. However, those students are the exception. We're going to use this Kindergarten Sun image that is already in our students' heads as a starting point for building a mental model for light.

An example activity sheet is shown in Activity 4.1, where students develop the Kindergarten Sun Model of Light and then use it to describe pictorially various situations. Using this activity, we have set-up a framework based on coaching that has the student use their own experiences and ideas to build a model for light "rays." Like the last activity, this activity could be used in both the first- and the fourth-grade classroom. The student is also asked to expand on their new knowledge of model

Figure 4.2 A fourth grader's representation of the sun.

building to make new representations for different content (in this case, heat).

Activity 4.1 A Mental Model for Light

Part I: A Mental Model for Light

Science Practice: Developing Models

In your science notebook, draw a picture of the sun. Share your picture with your group and discuss what is similar about your pictures. Be prepared to present your picture of the sun to the class and discuss what feature of your picture tells you that the sun is creating light.

Wait for further instructions from the teacher before moving to the next part. Your teacher will discuss the idea of models and your pictures of the sun.

Part II: Using a Model for Light

Science Practice: Using Models
In your science notebook, draw two pictures of a light bulb. For one of the pictures, show that the light bulb is turned on and creating light. How can you use the ray model of light previously discussed to do this?

Part III: Making Representations

Science Practice: Developing and Using Models
In your science notebook, draw two pictures of soup bowls filled with soup. For one of the pictures, show that the soup is hot.

In the Kindergarten Sun Ray Model of Light, straight beams of light emanate from a light source in all directions. Notice that we have led the student to discover for themselves the first line of content in the notebook from Figure 4.1: "Light travels in a straight line away from the light source." Instead of telling the student that bit of knowledge, students use their own experiences and thoughts to *construct* knowledge, instead. There are two things happening now, instead of just content memorization: (1) students are learning what models are and how they are developed, and (2) they are learning the underlying content knowledge through the practice of model building.

Figure 4.3(a) shows an actual student-generated result for Part II of the activity, where the student is seen using a ray model of light to pictorially represent a light bulb turned off and on. Objects that create their own light have straight lines emanating in all directions from the source. Objects that do not create their own light, or that are turned off, do not have such rays. (*Aside:* This pictorial representation is not completely accurate and would be tested and explored in more depth in a middle school or high school activity. The Physics Education Research group at Rutgers University has an excellent activity that they have developed that does exactly this [Etkina, 2013].)

These student-generated images serve as an excellent jumping-off point for discussing models, which provides the necessary explicit instruction and reflection. Does the sun actually look like this? Do we see individual little rays coming off its surface? No, but light itself is impossible to draw since it isn't like regular stuff. We have to come up with some sort of

Figure 4.3 A fourth grader coming up with representations for (a) light, and (b) the "hot" over a bowl of soup.

representation that we can draw that says, "I'm a ball of light!" The best part is, young children have already done this in their own heads. When we use ideas that students already have, then they "own" those ideas. They don't see this model for light as something given to them by the expert, but more as an idea that they came up with as a useful tool for representing and understanding light.

Can students come up with their own useful mental models? We use Part III of the activity as a formative assessment of the student's mental model-building ability. Figure 4.3(b) shows a student-generated result for Part III of the activity, where the student expands on the practice of building mental models to pictorially represent a hot cup of soup. We see in Figure 4.3(b) the student representing the hot cup of soup by using squiggly lines. Of course, we don't see actual squiggly lines over hot soup, but the air over the soup does look a little wiggly, which is most likely where this representation is coming from. In a future lesson on refraction, we can actually revisit this example, since the wiggly looking air is a direct result of changes in the refractive index due to differences in surrounding air temperature. For our purposes immediately, though, we are having the student apply the practice to another context to assess their ability to practice modeling. Once again, we are demonstrating to the student that the practice will be made to count through this type of low-stakes formative assessment.

Developing a Predictive Physical Model

The Kindergarten Sun Ray Model of Light is an example of using existing student experiences and ideas and building on them to construct a useful mental model. However, we still have to answer the first question I posed above: How does a scientist actually develop a physical model that can be used to predict new behaviors. Without knowing the process used by the scientist, we can't hope to simulate that process in the classroom. I'm going to answer this question through an example. Specifically, we'll look at an activity that can be done in the classroom that uses the ray mental model for light and leads the student toward building a predictive physical model for the reflection of these light rays off mirrors and off other objects, allowing those objects to be seen.

We'll start by having students make simple observations of light reflection. After some basic observation, they will design and implement what is called an "observation experiment," that is a more formal investigation of variable response to change. In this case, the student will systematically change the incoming angle of a beam of light with respect to the mirror face and measure the reflected beam. The student can then recognize a pattern that leads to a hypothesis about the reflection of light off a mirror.

This is the process scientists use to come up with hypotheses that we will mimic in our classrooms.

An example activity sheet is shown in Activity 4.2. I'm going to leave the checklist for this activity as an exercise for you, the reader. In Part I, students construct a simple device that produces a thin beam of light, approximating a light "ray." They then aim the light beam at a plane mirror and sketch the resulting reflection for several different orientations of the mirror. We have students complete this component in a scientific notebook. The students observe that the reflected beam of light will change direction as the orientation of the mirror changes. You will work with the students to articulate this observation in both oral and written communication. Figure 4.7 shows an example of student work for this part of the activity.

Activity 4.2 Ray Model of Light and Reflection

Part I: Observing Reflection Off a Plane Mirror

Science Practice: Asking Questions and Making Observations

Your group is going to build and use a simple device that makes a beam of light. This beam of light will allow your group to investigate light reflection. Figure 4.4. shows the device. It is made up of a flashlight and a piece of cardboard with a narrow slit. Build this device with the materials you have been given. Make sure it produces a very thin beam of light. (*Note to teacher:* You may wish to construct the cardboard pieces beforehand.)

Figure 4.4 An example of what your completed beam-producing device will look like.

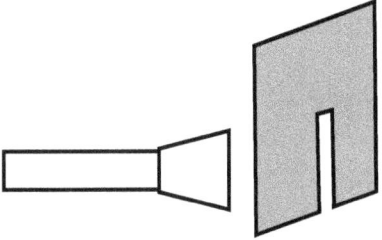

Aim the beam of light at the mirror and observe what happens. First, aim the beam directly at the mirror. Next, turn the mirror and observe what happens to the beam of light. Each member of your group should take a turn playing with the mirror and light beam.

Document your observations in your scientific notebook using both pictures and words. As a group, write one or two sentences that explains what you have observed.

After completing this part wait for further instruction from the teacher before moving to the next part. One representative from your group will present to the class during a class conference.

Part II: Using a Protractor to Measure Angles

Science Skill: Measuring Angles

Scientists must learn skills to make measurements. In this part, you will learn the skill of measuring an angle using a protractor. Watch as your teacher shows you how to make an angle measurement. We will use this skill in the next part.

Figure 4.5 shows two angles. Measure the angles using the protractor. Everyone in your group should complete this task. Compare your results with the other members of your group.

Part III: An Observation Experiment for Reflection Off Mirrors

Science Practice: Planning and Conducting Investigations/Developing and Using Models

Design and conduct an experiment that compares the incoming angle of a beam of light to the angle the reflected beam makes with a mirror. What variable will you control (independent variable)? Which variable will you measure (dependent variable)? Document the experiment in your science notebook. Summarize your results using a table.

Figure 4.5 Measure the size of the angles shown using a protractor.

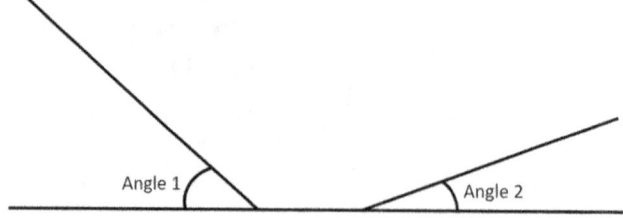

Figure 4.6 SCUBA Steve shines a flashlight on a fish. How do the flashlight's "rays" get back to Steve's eyes?

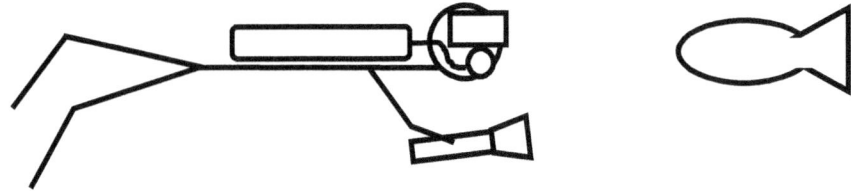

Part IV: Using the Ray Model and Reflection

Science Practice: Developing and Using Models

Figure 4.6 above shows SCUBA Steve swimming in a dark cave underwater. SCUBA Steve has a flashlight. Using a straight edge (like a ruler), draw several "rays" of light coming from the flashlight and hitting the fish. Show how the light could be reflected off the fish and enter SCUBA Steve's eye.

Follow-up question: Would SCUBA Steve be able to see the tail of the fish? Create an argument using evidence.

Figure 4.7 An example from a student's science notebook on the reflection of light off plane mirrors.

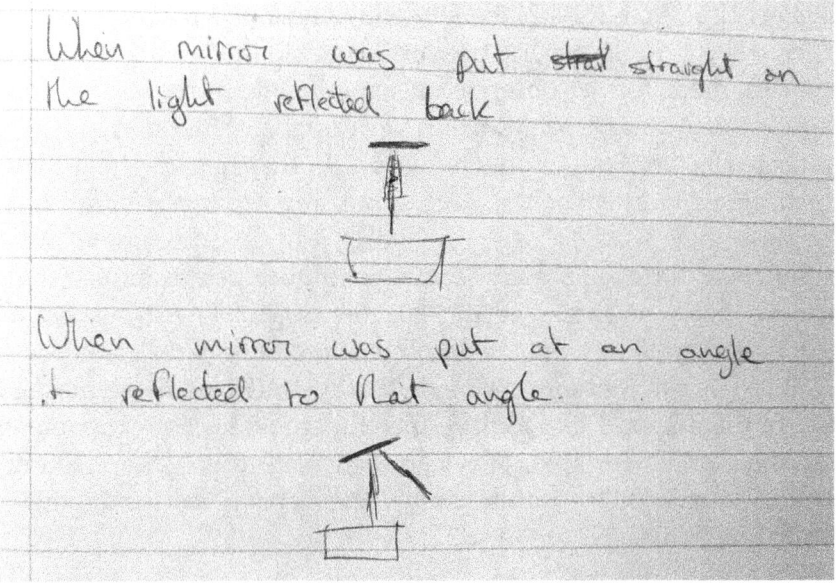

In Part II, the use of a protractor is modeled, so that students learn the skill of measuring angles. As we discussed in Chapter 2, domain-specific skill development is definitely necessary, but should not be confused with development of science practice abilities. In this particular instance, we need to introduce students to a specific measurement skill in order to make formal measurements for the next part of the activity. First, the teacher (you!) goes through the process of measuring an angle using a protractor in front of the whole class. Then, the students use a protractor to measure two angles provided for them on the activity sheet.

Planning and Carrying Out Observation Experiments

Next, we are going to have the students plan and conduct a more formal investigation. Investigations can be as simple as formal observations of the world around the scientist, up to systematic studies across multiple variables. The sophistication of the investigations should increase as the student progresses through the grade levels. The student must learn to make observations, plan and conduct experiments that test hypotheses, and implement investigations that can solve problems. The two types of investigations we're going to talk about in this chapter are observation experiments and testing experiments. Observation experiments lead to models/hypotheses. Testing experiments test models/hypotheses. We start with the observation experiment.

In Part II of Activity 4.2, the students developed the skills they need to carry out a simple observation experiment. In Part III, the students design this more formal observation experiment to investigate how the angle that the incoming beam makes with respect to the mirror will affect the reflected beam. First, students discuss in their groups how they will perform the experiment. Then, each group reports to the entire class on the process they want to use. You will guide this discussion, working with the class to develop a consensus procedure. An example would be aiming the beam at angles of 10°, 30°, 50°, and 70° with respect to the mirror, and then sketching the incoming and reflected beams for each. Then, students can measure the angle that the reflected beam makes with respect to the mirror. I like to have the students do these experiments on a large sheet of white paper. They can easily set-up the equipment on the paper, and sketch the resulting beams, transferring the results into their scientific notebooks.

Figure 4.8 shows a picture of (a) the experimental set-up and (b) an image of student work in their scientific notebook. Notice that the student has organized their results in a table. After students have collected results, you will want to model for the students how to organize these data into tables, similar to the way the results are organized in Figure 4.8b. I then like to have a representative from each group write their group's table of results on the board, so that we can then discuss and compare each group's results. From this discussion, the students are able to recognize the very simple pattern: The incoming beam angle is roughly equal to the reflected beam angle. After all of the groups have written their results on the board, they should now be able to tell you the pattern, and therefore the model they can use for reflection. It is important that the students articulate the model themselves, so that they "own" it as opposed to having it dictated to them.

This type of experiment and pattern recognition mimics the process scientists use to come up with models and hypotheses. In Chapter 1, we

Figure 4.8 (a) A picture of the experimental set-up devised by the student. (continues on next page)

Figure 4.8 (b) The student's scientific notebook showing their plan for and results from the investigation.

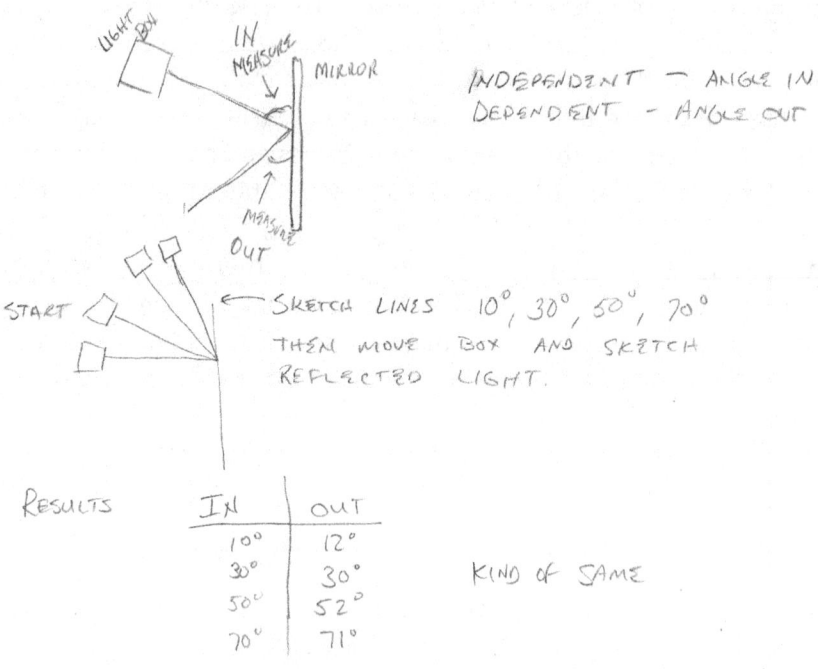

talked about science as being composed of both inductive and deductive components. Scientists make simple observations, and from these observations, they are able to determine relevant variables. In this case, the students observe that the reflected beam direction changes with orientation of the mirror. Once the relevant variables are determined, the scientist can then develop a more rigorous *observation experiment*, or what science education researcher Eugenia Etkina calls a *hypothesis-generating experiment* (Etkina et al., 2010). By recognizing patterns, scientists are then able to use inductive reasoning to develop a model or hypothesis for the physical system. In the next section, we will look at a hypothesis-testing experiment (more simply called a testing experiment), where deductive reasoning is used to test a model or hypothesis of a physical system.

Now, that we have a hypothesis for how light behaves when bouncing off a mirror, how do we extend this model to understanding that light reflecting off objects allows those objects to be seen? Part IV of Activity 4.2 accomplishes this by replacing the mirror with an object (we've used a fish to tie this activity to the underwater cave diver video I described earlier). We have students complete this part individually as a formative assessment of their ability to use a model to understand content. The student can draw rays of light emanating from the flashlight that reflect off the fish and direct back to the SCUBA diver's eye.

Let's look back at what we have done over the previous two activities. First, we have used the students' previous experience to help them develop a mental model of light that they own. We didn't dictate the model to them. They created it themselves. Next, we used that model to understand how light reflects off objects. We started with the simple case of a plane mirror and used a more formal observation experiment to learn that "rays" of light reflect off mirrors at the same angle in which they strike the mirror. The students made the observation, designed the experiment (with coaching), and recognized the pattern themselves. They constructed their own new knowledge using the practices of science. This more formal model for light and its reflection was then used to address the specific NGSS performance expectation. You should also notice the close ties between the practices of developing models and planning and conducting investigations. Scientists need observations to make models.

Before moving on to hypothesis-testing experiments, let's look back at the first grade classroom. I want to briefly discuss how we might address the following NGSS performance expectation.

Students who demonstrate understanding can

- **(1-PS4–2)** *Make observations* to construct an evidence-based account that objects in darkness can be seen only when illuminated

Table 4.5 shows an example of the checklist for an activity that would address this student performance expectation. Let's think about the types of observations we could realistically get a student to make that would provide evidence that objects in darkness can be seen only when illuminated. The first observation experiment we could do, and the easiest to implement, would be simply having the students close their eyes. Place an object in front of them, have them close their eyes. Can they see the object? How could they tell that it's still there? By touching it?

Another simple observation experiment we could do requires a small amount of inexpensive equipment: a shoe box. Put a small hole in the top of

TABLE 4.5 SAMPLE CHECKLIST FOR AN APPRENTICESHIP-BASED ACTIVITY APPLIED TO THE PRACTICE OF MAKING OBSERVATIONS ABOUT THE BEHAVIOR OF LIGHT.

Checklist	Description
Identify the practice and content	A student that demonstrates understanding can *make observations* to construct an evidence-based account that objects in darkness can be seen only when illuminated.
Identify how the student will construct knowledge	For the first grader, we will coach them toward the design of an observation experiment that answers a research question. Specifically, given a box with eye holes cut out and an unknown object inside, what observations might the student make to answer the question?
Define the community the student will work within	Students will work in small teams to determine the observation they will make with the available materials. We will have groups discuss with the class what observations they will make and what they think will happen. The class will decide as a whole the procedure to use, and then each team will make the observation, reporting back in a whole-class conference.
Define the explicit instruction to be given	We will be explicit about the practice of answering scientific questions through observations. We will be explicit in describing what observations can tell us.
Identify how you will encourage reflection	Some objects can be seen without an external source of illumination. An excellent follow-up would be placing glow sticks in the box and discussing the difference between objects that make their own light and objects that need reflected light to be seen.
Define how the activity will be made to count	I want you to think about how you might formatively assess whether or not your first graders are learning how to make observations. Can they articulate their observations verbally? Can they sketch their observations?

a shoe box and a larger hole in the side. Place an item in the box and cover the larger hole. Have the students look in the box through the small hole on top. Can they identify the object? Now, open the larger hole and allow light to shine into the box. The students should recognize that the object can now be seen and connect that to the introduction of light though the larger hole.

These are simple observations that students can make that directly answer some of the scientific questions we got them to ask previously. When designing your own activities, it's important to think in this way: How can I get the student to *discover* the content I want them to know? This is far more effective than just telling them the content.

Planning and Carrying Out Testing Experiments

Observation experiments are one type of investigation. The other type we'll discuss is the testing experiment. Once the scientist has made observations, recognized patterns, and formed a hypothesis based on those patterns, then the scientist needs to devise experiments that test their hypothesis. After all, a good model of reality is predictive, meaning we can use it to predict behavior previously unseen. In this final section, I will describe a short activity that has students test their new model of light reflection off plane mirrors, and the formal structure you can use to force students to reflect on their reasoning and practice.

First, let's look at the final student performance expectation from Table 4.2.

Students who demonstrate understanding can

- *Design and conduct an investigation* that tests the hypothesis that rays of light reflect off mirrors at the same angle in which they hit the mirror

Let's imagine this is one of the first times you will have had students in your class design and conduct a testing experiment. If this is the case, then you will need to properly scaffold the process for students, so that they can learn how a good testing experiment is designed. An effective way of scaffolding this process is by using the explicit construct of what biology education professor Anton Lawson calls the "If . . . and . . . then . . ." (IAT) statement (Moore, 2012). Lawson presents a series of activities that lead students through the process of constructing good IAT statements in various fields of knowledge in an excellent paper listed in the references section of this chapter (Lawson, 2000). In this way, the hypothetico-deductive reasoning pattern we discussed in Chapter 1 is being made explicit. We want students to design an experiment that would address the question "do rays of light reflect off mirrors at the same angle in which they hit the mirror?" (Notice this is an example of a scientific question!) We can formalize the process by forcing students to construct an appropriate IAT statement that is specifically designed to potentially falsify or support a claim.

First, what is an IAT statement? Table 4.6 describes the basic construction of the IAT statement, which we describe and model for the students. The basic structure is as follows:

IF a hypothesis, AND we do this experiment, THEN this would be the result. AND/BUT the actual result was this, THEREFORE the hypothesis is supported/falsified.

TABLE 4.6 MAKING HYPOTHETICO-DEDUCTIVE REASONING FOR LIGHT REFLECTION EXPLICIT THROUGH THE IAT STATEMENT.

If...	Hypothesis	Light reflects off a plane mirror at the same angle at which it strikes the mirror.
And...	Testing experiment	We aim a beam of light at an angle of 25° with respect to the mirror.
Then...	Result if hypothesis is true	The reflected beam will also be at an angle of 25° with respect to the mirror.
And/But...	Actual result of testing experiment	The beam did reflect at a 25° angle.
Therefore...	Conclusion	The hypothesis is supported.

By working with students to construct statements like this for their hypotheses, we force them to do the following:

1. to explicitly state their hypothesis,
2. to articulate the testing experiment they intend to do,
3. to think about what prediction the hypothesis should lead to, and
4. to reflect on what the evidence tells them.

Let's look at our specific example. The observation experiment from the previous section led the student to the hypothesis that light reflects off a plane mirror at the same angle at which it strikes the mirror. How might we test this? We can assign an arbitrary incoming angle, preferably one for which we haven't yet made an observation, and then have the students measure the reflected angle. For example, the hypothesis tells us that an incoming beam of light at an angle of 25° should reflect off the mirror at an angle of 25°.

Students can now work in groups to conduct the experiment. You might wish to provide them with a printed worksheet having the location of the mirror and a line representing the incoming beam at the appropriate angle. Then, the students can make a prediction by using the protractor to sketch where the reflected beam should go based on the hypothesis. Once they have made a prediction, they can place their flashlight device such that the beam aligns with the printed incoming beam line. If the resulting real reflected beam lines up with their prediction, then they can conclude that the hypothesis is supported.

Summary

In this chapter, I have shown examples of how to teach content through the practices of asking questions, developing and using models, and planning and conducting investigations. Specifically, I described a "traditional" lesson on the reflection of light and showed how to teach the same content through practices. We discussed the checklist for practice-centric activities and how to use it, with a couple of explicit examples. This should serve as a foundation of knowledge that you can use to begin designing your own practice-centric lessons.

The following is a brief summary of the main points:

- Teaching-by-telling does not teach practices.
- The representations of the physical world that you use in your class need to be developed by the student and not implied.
- Students should be taught to distinguish between scientific and non-scientific questions.
- When a student constructs their own mental models, they "own" them, automatically instilling in that student an expert-like view of science.
- Students can come up with their own predictive models using observation experiments and pattern recognition.
- Testing experiments test hypotheses and help develop reasoning patterns.

References

Alesandrini, K., & Larson, L. (2002). Teachers bridge to constructivism. *The Clearing House, 75*(3), 118–121.

Box, G. E. (1979). Robustness in the strategy of scientific model building. In R. Launer & G. Wilkinson (Eds.), *Robustness in Statistics*. New York, NY: Academic Press.

Etkina, E. (2013). *Using Physics to Help Students Develop Scientific Habits of Mind*. Retrieved from ICPE 2013 Conference: http://icpe2013.org/presentations/EugeniaEtkina.pdf

Etkina, E., Karelina, A., Ruibal-Villasenor, M., Rosengrant, D., Jordan, R., & Hmelo-Silver, C. (2010). Design and reflection help students develop scientific abilities: Learning in introductory physics laboratories. *Journal of Learning Sciences, 19*, 54–98.

Hake, R. R. (1998). Interactive-engagement vs traditional methods: A six-thousand student survey of mechanics test data for introductory physics courses. *American Journal of Physics, 66*, 64–74.

Lawson, A. E. (2000). The generality of hypothetico-deductive reasoning: Making scientific thinking explicit. *American Biology Teacher, 62*, 482.

Lord, T., & Orkwiszewski, T. (2006). Moving from didactic to inquiry-based instruction in a science laboratory. *The Biology Teacher, 68*(6), 342–345.

Moore, J. C. (2012). Transitional to formal operational: Using authentic research experiences to get non-science students to think more like scientists. *European Journal of Physics Education, 3*(4), 1–12.

National Research Council. (2012). *A Framework for K–12 Science Education: Practices, Crosscutting Concepts, and Core Ideas.* Washington, DC: The National Academies Press.

NGSS Lead States. (2013a). APPENDIX E—Progressions Within the Next Generation Science Standards. In N. L. States (Ed.), *Next Generation Science Standards: For States, by States.* Washington, DC: The National Academies Press.

NGSS Lead States. (2013b). *Next Generation Science Standards: For States, by States.* Washington, DC: The National Academies Press.

Rees, M. (2011, September 19). Britain needs schools for science. *The Guardian.*

South Carolina Department of Education. (2014). *South Carolina Academic Standards and Performance Indicators for Science.* Columbia, SC: State Board of Education.

5

Interpreting Results and Teaching Abstract Concepts

"The goal of science is the construction of theories that provide explanatory accounts of the world. A theory becomes accepted when it has multiple lines of empirical evidence and greater explanatory power of phenomena than previous theories."
—A Framework for K–12 Education (2012, p. 52)

Once scientists complete the investigation, they then have data to interpret. This is the second science practice dimension. To build an explanatory model of how the world works, the scientist must first record, analyze, and interpret the data. Patterns and relationships between variables are more easily recognized in well-arranged data. Once these patterns become clear, the scientist then uses mathematical and computational thinking to quantitatively model the phenomenon. These quantitative mathematical and/or computational models are used to make predictions that can then be tested or used to solve some problem. Finally, the scientist must explain the phenomenon by answering the following question: Why does this happen? Explanations are built on evidence and reason. Students use investigation to gather the evidence, and they use interpretation to justify explanations.

In this chapter, we'll look at some simple examples of interpreting data gathered through investigations done in the classroom. Specifically, I'll show you real-world examples from the teaching and learning of energy. We'll discuss the difficulty students have wrapping their brains around abstract concepts like energy, and how we can build understanding by first making these types of ideas more concrete. We'll start with the elementary school classroom, where students interpret data qualitatively using easily observable examples. Then, we'll progress into the middle school classroom where interpretations and explanations become more quantitative. Specifically, I'll show you a learning progression you can go through to teach students about motion energy and energy in waves. To gather some of the data, we'll revisit some ideas from the previous chapter.

As with the previous chapter, I'll use the checklist for activity development from Chapter 2 as a guide, and I'll also take advantage of the framework for developing assessable curriculum discussed in Chapter 3. I'll show you some simple rubrics for assessing performance expectations in the science practice dimension of interpretation, and I'll demonstrate real student work and how it was assessed. Once again, it's important to realize that this is not intended as a chapter about teaching energy specifically, but a chapter about teaching the practices of interpretation within some context. I don't want you to focus too much on the content. I want you to think about how the content and activities are being used to teach the practices. Even though your specific content may differ, the approach to teaching through practice will be the same.

Interpreting Observations

The *Framework* states the following about the ultimate goal of science:

> The goal of science is the construction of theories that provide explanatory accounts of the world. A theory becomes accepted when it has multiple lines of empirical evidence and greater explanatory power of phenomena than previous theories.
> (National Research Council, 2012, p. 52)

I placed this quote at the beginning of this chapter for a very important reason. Ultimately, teachers and students have a tendency to get so caught up in the excitement of the investigation that we tend to spend little time delving into interpretation and sense-making. Experiments are fun, after all, and data analysis just sounds so dreadfully boring. However, the ultimate goal of science is to make sense of the world. That is to say, the goal is to create *explanations* for why the world behaves the way it does and to *build models* that we can use to understand and to make our world better. We need to spend at least equal time focusing on the abilities that make that happen.

Furthermore, sense-making is far from boring. In fact, as I mentioned in the introduction to this book, almost *all* children are incredibly curious about the world around them. They are immediately drawn to science because of its power to explain the mysteries all around them, and children crave explanations. As a species, we're hardwired to want to make sense of our world. When approached correctly, interpretation can be just as fun as and even more rewarding to the student than the "play" of experiments, especially when they get to use their own data. They *own* their explanations and sense-making!

The science practice dimension of interpretation is where this sense-making happens. Table 5.1 details the science practices outlined by the *Framework* that I have grouped into the interpretation dimension (National

TABLE 5.1 SCIENCE PRACTICES WITHIN THE DIMENSION OF INTERPRETATION.

Science Practice	Description
Analyze and interpret data	While a scientist conducts an investigation, he or she collects data. These data must be arranged and presented in a way that allows the scientist to easily recognize patterns and relationships. As students progress, they must learn how to tabulate data, construct graphical representations and visualizations, and complete statistical analyses.
Use mathematics and computational thinking	Scientists use mathematics and computation to model the patterns and relationships they find through data analyzation and interpretation. These quantitative mathematical and computational models are used to make predictions that can be tested or used. Students must learn how to qualitatively and quantitatively express relationships as mathematical expressions and/or computer simulations through code.
Construct explanations and design solutions	Patterns in data are usually the result of some physical process that can be explained. The *Framework* states the following: "The goal of science is the construction of theories that provide explanatory accounts of the world" (National Research Council, 2012). The student will use data and the patterns and relationships found in the data to construct explanations. These explanations answer the question *why*.

Research Council, 2012). The interpretation dimension consists of the following practices:

1. Analyzing and interpreting data
2. Using mathematics and computational thinking
3. Constructing explanations and designing solutions

Once the investigation is complete, then the data collected by the scientist must be arranged and presented in a way that allows the scientist to easily recognize patterns and relationships. These patterns are the basis on which sense-making happen (pattern recognition is also a cross-cutting concept in the NGSS.) If you wish to create scientists, then you must teach your students how to tabulate data, construct graphical representations and visualizations, and complete statistical analyses so that patterns and relationships can be discovered.

When data are represented well, then the scientists can use mathematics and computation to model the patterns and relationships they find. These quantitative and/or qualitative models are used to make predictions that can be tested or used to solve problems. Your students must learn how to describe relationships as mathematical expressions and/or computer simulations. Furthermore, they must learn how to use these models to make falsifiable predictions.

Finally, patterns in data are usually the result of some physical process that can be explained. By representing data properly, patterns can be discovered that we can mathematically or computationally model. These models form the foundation of an explanation. These explanations answer the question *why*. Why does nature behave in this way? What evidence do we have to suggest that this explanation is correct? As the *Framework* says, this is the goal of scientists, and therefore the goal of science teaching is to teach students how to get to this point.

Energy: Teaching Abstract Concepts Through Practice

For examples of teaching interpretation, we're going to look at some sample classroom activities on the topic of energy from the Disciplinary Core Ideas (DCIs) in physical science. For the example of energy that we're going to use, the relevant DCIs are *PS3.A Definitions of energy* and *PS3.B Conservation of energy and energy transfer*. The learning progression throughout the grade levels is summarized in Table 5.2 (NGSS Lead States, 2013a).

The student's first exposure to energy during early elementary grade levels is when they make observations of the Earth's surface warming due to the emergence of the sun. Although we don't quite refer to it as energy necessarily at this stage, we are laying the groundwork for a phenomenon that is transferable from one object to another.

In the upper-elementary levels, students learn that moving objects have energy and this energy can be transformed from one form to another form. In our examples later in this chapter, we'll mostly focus on energy and motion. In middle school, students begin tracking changes in and transfers of energy. In the examples we'll discuss later in this chapter, students discover a mathematical relationship between the kinetic energy of an object and the object's speed and mass, and learn about energy in waves.

Finally, in high school, a more sophisticated and abstract picture of energy emerges. Students learn how to quantify energy in many forms, conserve energy, and make predictions about the future state of objects based on a system's total energy composition and the energy state of the system's components.

Energy as a concept is actually very abstract. As an abstract concept, energy is a "thing" that exists in the scientist's thoughts, and although we can see the indirect consequences of energy, energy itself has no concrete existence that we can see and touch. Many of the concepts we teach in the sciences require a great deal of imagination to visualize. For example,

TABLE 5.2 DCI GRADE-LEVEL PROGRESSION FOR ENERGY, CONSERVATION OF ENERGY, AND TRANSFER OF ENERGY SUMMARIZED FROM THE NGSS APPENDIX E: PROGRESSIONS WITHIN THE NEXT GENERATION SCIENCE STANDARDS (NGSS LEAD STATES, 2013A).

Grade Level	Progression
K–2	Energy is transferred from the sun to the Earth, warming its surface. (We don't yet call it energy.)
3–5	Moving objects have energy, and energy can be transformed from one form to another form.
6–8	Changes in and transfers of energy can be tracked, and kinetic energy depends on the physical properties of objects such as speed and mass.
9–12	The total energy of a system is conserved, and energy transfer can be described and predicted.

the atomic structure is something that can't be seen directly. Strands of DNA are too small for all but the most expensive microscopes, and even then lack resolution. Can we really fathom the distance between the stars when our day-to-day experience with distance is measured in miles or kilometers. What does "energy" look like? Can you touch it?

The education theorist Anton Lawson describes three types of concepts in science: concrete, hypothetical, and theoretical (Lawson, Alkhoury, Benford, Clark, & Falconer, 2000; Lawson, Clark, et al., 2000). Concrete concepts are those ideas that have directly observable exemplars. Hypothetical concepts have observable exemplars, but are on scales far outside the everyday experiences of the scientist. Theoretical concepts have no directly observable exemplars.

For example, when creating a taxonomy of species of fish, we can directly observe the differences in the fishes on which the taxonomy is based. The student conducting an investigation on a pendulum and how the period depends on the mass and string length can directly observe (mass and length) or experience (time) all three variables. These are examples of concrete concepts.

A student investigating the shrinking cells of an onion skin in saltwater can see the cells and observe their size using a microscope; however, students have to use significant imaginative faculties to conceive of the concept of un-observable charged water molecules leaving the cell due to some spooky attraction to charged sodium chloride molecules in the water. The student can directly observe the cells shrinking, but the causal agent is not directly observable. This would be an example of a hypothetical concept, where real stuff is transferring from the cell to the water, but the scale is outside of our direct perception. Similarly, strands of DNA, electrons and protons, and the size of Jupiter are all things that we could directly grasp were we a lot smaller or a lot bigger.

Finally, let's think about that spooky attraction between the water and salt molecules. Force as a concept has no observable exemplar no matter how small or large a size scale we could perceive. It isn't a "thing" like a cell at all. Similarly, energy has no physical substance. Both force and energy are concepts completely made up by scientists. They are useful concepts because they explain behavior we can observe, such as changing speeds of objects, objects getting hotter, and massive stuff requiring more effort to move. That's why scientists made them up. However, they cannot be directly observed. Ever. These are examples of theoretical concepts.

If you look through the NGSS DCIs while thinking about the distinction between these types of concepts, you'll find that a lot of the science content we are expected to teach is either hypothetical or theoretical. Most of our work with elementary school students is confined to the concrete. However, as the student progresses through the grade levels, the way we approach content becomes more and more abstract, requiring greater and greater imagination and visualization ability to understand.

Students have a great deal of difficulty with hypothetical and theoretical constructs. Multiple studies have shown that a student's ability to understand abstract science content depends on their developmental level and scientific reasoning ability. Specifically, Lawson used the onion cell example I mentioned above to show that success at imagining hypothetical concepts is correlated with scientific reasoning ability, which is measurably low even at the college age-level (Lawson, Clark, et al., 2000). In the physical sciences, Coletta and Phillips observed a strong correlation between content learning in the domain of forces (you can't see a force) and scientific reasoning ability, where weaker reasoners learned less during instruction than strong reasoners, even with research-verified reformed pedagogy (Coletta & Phillips, 2005). My own research has found that pre- and in-service science teachers more readily learn concrete topics, such as light bulb circuits, compared to abstract concepts, such as motion and energy (Moore, 2012). Learning gains have weak correlation with cognitive ability for concrete topics, and strong correlation for abstract content (Moore & Rubbo, 2012).

Imagining both hypothetical and theoretical concepts is considered to be a *thresholded* ability. A threshold to learning exists for content when the learner significantly struggles to understand up until reaching a certain cognitive level, at which point the concept becomes relatively easy and obvious to the student. This can be thought of as the "Eureka!" moment. For example, my research with colleagues has shown that mathematical thinking is exceptionally difficult for students up to a certain cognitive level (Moore & Slisko, 2017). After reaching the threshold, mathematical thinking and pattern recognition becomes significantly easier. This is important for this chapter because we'll be dealing with energy (theoretical) and the science practice of mathematical and computational thinking.

The point in all of this is that you need to recognize that your students *will* have great difficulty wrapping their minds around these types of concepts. You and the "weird" students we talked about in the introduction might be naturally good at the hypothetical/theoretical, but most students are not. It may be easy for you and the "weird" students to recognize patterns, but most of your class will require significant intervention. It's easy to leave our thinking and mental models implied, assuming the student will just pick them up. That won't necessarily happen. Being mindful of this will help you in your teaching of science.

For example, the ray model of light we talked about in the previous chapter is a theoretical concept. Light doesn't actually look like straight arrows. Merely plunking down some arrows like the visualization we saw in Figure 4.1 isn't a very good way of teaching students about light, because the physical reality of light is abstract, requiring the student to theorize about its existence and imagine useful ways of representing it. Most students can't internalize this visualization without significant intervention. They can picture a chair or an octopus in their minds because they've seen chairs and octopuses. Chairs are real, concrete things they can touch. Light beams? Not so much.

Then how do we teach abstract hypothetical and theoretical concepts? There are two approaches to dealing with this type of content (Moore, 2017):

1. build off students' existing ideas, and/or
2. begin with more concrete manifestations of the concept and build from there.

We already looked at an example of the first approach in Chapter 4 where we had the students build a mental model for light based on their existing ideas of how to visualize light. This was the Kindergarten Sun Ray Model of Light. We also produced a concrete physical manifestation of the ray model with the ray box we constructed in Activity 4.2. That's an example of the second approach. Similarly, in this chapter we're going to look at teaching abstract content (through practice, of course!) by building from a more concrete base.

For example, Table 5.3 shows a possible learning progression for energy from motion and energy in waves. In particular, we start the learning progression by having students participate in an investigation where they rub their hands together at varying speeds. With our elementary school class, we build a qualitative explanation from the observations in this

TABLE 5.3 AN EXAMPLE LEARNING PROGRESSION FOR ENERGY FROM MOTION AND ENERGY IN WAVES. BOLDED LABELS REPRESENT PERFORMANCE EXPECTATIONS TAKEN DIRECTLY FROM THE NGSS (NGSS LEAD STATES, 2013A).

Content	NGSS-based Performance Expectation
Energy from motion (qualitative)	Students who demonstrate understanding can ♦ *Conduct an investigation* on the relationship between the motion of your hands rubbing together, and heat generated ♦ *Construct and interpret graphical displays of data* to qualitatively describe the relationship between motion and energy ♦ **(4-PS3–1)** *Use evidence to construct an explanation* relating the speed of an object to the energy of that object
Energy from motion (quantitative)	Students who demonstrate understanding can ♦ **(MS-PS3–1)** *Construct and interpret graphical displays of data* to describe the relationships of kinetic energy to the mass of an object and to the speed of an object
Energy in waves	Students who demonstrate understanding can ♦ *Plan and conduct investigations* to determine the relationship between the amplitude of a wave and its energy, and the frequency of a wave and its energy ♦ **(MS-PS4–1)** *Use mathematical representations to describe* a simple model for waves that includes how the amplitude of a wave is related to the energy in a wave

investigation. From there, middle school students would use mathematical thinking to develop a quantitative relationship between speed and energy. These ideas can then be applied to the even more abstract concept of waves.

Notice that the entire progression begins with a very concrete act: Students rubbing their hands together. They can directly experience the relative values of heat that they feel as a function of how fast they rub their hands together. We are making the theoretical concept of energy more concrete. This allows the students to begin the construction of a mental model, which will allow them to practice with the content and therefore understand. Whenever possible, bring the abstract into the concrete world.

In the following series of example activities, we're going to look at interpreting data in the context of energy. Data interpretation itself is an ability that requires the student to imagine outside of the firmly concrete domain. Therefore, we'll keep these lessons in mind as we go through the sample activities.

Interpreting Real Data: Making, Visualizing, and Explaining Observations

Activity 5.1 shows a series of activities that you can do in the classroom that starts by connecting the theoretical concept of energy to a concrete, directly measurable phenomenon (warm hands), and finishes with students using evidence they have gathered to address the following NGSS performance expectation (NGSS Lead States, 2013b):

> 4-PS3–1. Use evidence to construct an explanation relating the speed of an object to the energy of that object.

Activity 5.1 Using Evidence to Explain the Relationship Between Speed and Energy

Part I: Investigating Energy and Motion

Science Practice: Conducting Investigations
You're interested in investigating how energy can be related to motion. You will do this by rubbing your hands together at various speeds. Start by having each member of the group rub their hands together slowly and then quickly.

What did you notice when you rubbed your hands together?

From this observation, come up with a way of measuring the energy. Also, come up with a way of measuring the speed of your hands. Your measurements only need to be qualitative, meaning you just need to be able to tell if you have more or less energy and speed than another measurement.

Record several observations by rubbing your hands together at four different speeds (slow, medium, fast, and superfast.) Also, record the energy you measure at these speeds (a little energy, more energy, a lot more energy, and super energy.)

Part II: Graphing Energy as a Result of Motion

Science Practice: Analyzing and Interpreting Data
You will now organize your data in a graph. A graph is a visual representation of your observations that will allow you to more easily see patterns and relationships.

Figure 5.1 The axes for a graph of energy vs. hand speed.

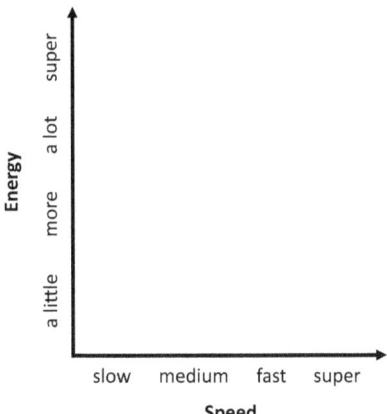

Figure 5.1 shows how you will set-up your graph, with the amount of energy as the dependent variable, and the speed of your hands as the independent variable.

Fill in the graph using your observations for the energy.

Part III: Explaining the Relationship

Science Practice: Constructing Explanations

Using your observations and your graph, you will now be able to explain the relationship between the speeds of objects, in this case your hands, and the energy.

From what you have done in the first two parts of this activity, write a statement that summarizes what you know about how the speed is related to the energy.

What evidence did you use to come up with this statement?

Can you think of other examples that provide more evidence?

In Part I, students observe that the palms of their hands get warmer as they rub their hands together. Using this observation, they conduct a short and simple investigation of the relationship between speed and energy. Notice that we are asking the student to determine how they intend to measure energy. Naturally, almost all of them will choose to measure how hot their hands get during rubbing as an indication of energy. Determining and articulating how a measurement will be made is a significant component of the science practice of planning and conducting investigations.

Once the students have recorded their observations, we move to Part II where the students now have data to visualize. If this is the first time you have worked with students in your classroom on graphs of data, then you will need to start off by modeling how it is done. In this case, Part II would be a modeled exercise. Otherwise, with more and more instruction, you should allow students more and more freedom to create their graphs.

Finally, in Part III, students interpret their graphs to explain the relationship between the speed of an object and the energy of the object. They do this by articulating a statement about the relationship such as the following:

"As the speed of an object increases its energy increases."

They then use evidence and reasoning to justify their statement. For example, you will work with students to build an explicit chain of reasoning that links the observations that they made to their statement about the relationship between energy and speed. An example of such a chain of reasoning is as follows:

1. As I moved my hands faster over each other, they got warmer.
2. Warmness is an indication of energy.
3. Therefore, as I moved my hands faster they had more energy.
4. Hands are objects.
5. As the speed of an object increases its energy increases.

It's important to follow-up with the entire group by having them think of other examples and observations from their experiences that they could draw on to support their statement. For example, falling off a bike moving slowly versus moving fast. Catching a baseball pitch. Does a fastball hurt your hand more? Does it make a louder thud in the glove? Again, pulling examples from the student's experience provides that student with ownership of the observation. The student *discovers* the link between speed and energy. Students *create their own* concrete understanding of energy: hot hands, scraped knees, and louder smashing sounds. They aren't being told science content by an expert, they are discovering science content through their own experiences and observations.

Let's think about how we might assess this activity by following the curriculum development framework from Chapter 3 and shown in

Figure 3.1. We've defined our learning goals using the structure of the NGSS performance expectations and laid out a learning progression, as shown in Table 5.3. We then designed a three-part activity that takes students through that learning progression. Now, we'll use the NGSS evidence statements to build a rubric for assessment. For example, Table 5.4 shows the generic evidence statements from the NGSS for using evidence to construct explanations.

However, in our three-part activity, students are actually using three science practices, instead of just the one practice provided in **4-PS3–1**. Example 5.1 shows a rubric we could use to assess the entire activity. The top level of the rubric is generic and is based on pieces of the NGSS evidence statements for each practice. The individual criterions are specific to the content we have the student investigating and interpreting.

TABLE 5.4 EVIDENCE STATEMENTS FOR USING EVIDENCE TO CONSTRUCT EXPLANATIONS. ADAPTED FROM NGSS LEAD STATES (2013B).

	The student
1	Articulates the explanation of phenomena
2	Identifies and describes the relevant evidence for the explanation
3	Uses reason to connect the evidence to the explanation

Example 5.1 Rubric for assessment of combined investigation and interpretation activity

Plans the investigation			
	Unsatisfactory	Needs Improvement	Satisfactory
Describes how the energy will be measured	The student does not describe how the energy will be measured.	The student describes how the energy will be measured, but is unclear.	The student describes how the energy will be measured, and it will result in a useful measurement.

(Continued)

Example 5.1 (Continued)

Conducts the investigation

	Unsatisfactory	Needs Improvement	Satisfactory
Makes and records observations according to the given plan	The student does not record observations.	The observations are made and recorded, but not according to the plan OR the record is unclear.	The student makes and records the observations according to the plan.

Organizing data

	Unsatisfactory	Needs Improvement	Satisfactory
Uses graphical displays to organize the data for speed and energy	The student does not organize the data.	The student organizes data in a graphical display, but there are errors, or the display is not clear.	The student organizes the data in a graphical display correctly and clearly.

Articulating the explanation of phenomena

	Unsatisfactory	Needs Improvement	Satisfactory
Articulates a statement that relates the energy to the speed	The student provides no written statement.	A statement is attempted, but it is either unclear or incorrect based on the evidence.	The student articulates a statement that correctly relates the energy to the speed based on the evidence.

Evidence

	Unsatisfactory	Needs Improvement	Satisfactory
Students identify and describe the relevant given evidence for the explanation.	No evidence is identified.	Evidence is provided, but it does not support the explanation.	Evidence that supports the explanation is provided.

You'll notice that in the learning progression, activity, and assessment, we were not confined to NGSS performance expectations, and we didn't focus only on a single science practice. As you grow more comfortable teaching through practice, you will begin to realize that the practices themselves don't have easily identifiable "borders." An observation experiment leading to a recognizable pattern necessarily becomes a lesson in argument from evidence and explanation construction. Working in a team to develop and use a model often requires abilities at analyzing data and using mathematics. In reality, the practices are intertwined and should be learned and taught this way.

Analyzing and Interpreting Data Quantitatively

Activity 5.1 was a qualitative activity for a fourth-grade class. As students progress through the grade levels, the practices stay the same, but their application becomes more sophisticated. In the previous example, we discussed students making qualitative measurements and graphing them qualitatively. The best they could do is tell whether something got bigger or smaller, but not by how much. In middle school, we start developing more sophisticated pattern recognition abilities. Therefore, we can begin to look at relationships more quantitatively.

Activity 5.2 uses simulated data to address the following NGSS performance expectation (NGSS Lead States, 2013b):

> **MS-PS3–1.** Construct and interpret graphical displays of data to describe the relationships of kinetic energy to the mass of an object and to the speed of an object.

Activity 5.2 Analyzing and Interpreting Data to Determine What Affects the Kinetic Energy of An Object

Part I: Graphical Displays of Data

Science Practice: Analyzing and Interpreting Data
Skills: using a computer to graph data
   (a) Speed and kinetic energy of a wagon

speed (m/s)	kinetic energy (J)
1	1
2	4
3	9
4	16

(b) mass and kinetic energy of a wagon mass (kg)	kinetic energy (J)
1	2
2	4
3	6
4	8

These tables provide data for (a) the kinetic energy of a wagon with a fixed mass going at different speeds, and (b) the kinetic energy of the same wagon going a fixed speed but with different masses.

Create a scatter plot graphical display for each set of data, where the kinetic energy is the dependent variable and the speed and mass are the independent variables.

Part II: Recognizing Patterns in Data

Science Practice: Analyzing and Interpreting Data
    If the mass of the wagon doubles, by how much does the kinetic energy go up?
    If the mass of the wagon triples, by how much does the kinetic energy go up?
    If the speed doubles, by how much does the kinetic energy go up?
    If the speed triples, by how much does the kinetic energy go up?
    Predict the kinetic energy of the wagon if it has a mass of 5 kg.

Predict the kinetic energy of the wagon if it has a speed of 5 m/s.

In Part I of this simple activity, students are given raw simulated data for the kinetic energy of a wagon having different masses and speeds. They then created a graphical display of the kinetic energy as a function of the mass, and then another display of the kinetic energy as a function of the speed. They do this using a computer and spreadsheet software. The use of software like this is a skill (as opposed to an ability); therefore, before completing this activity, you will want to have modeled how to use the spreadsheet software and how to create a basic two-dimensional scatter plot. This activity is an excellent opportunity for the student to begin independently practicing this skill.

    Figure 5.2 shows example graphs created by a student for both relationships. Good graphical displays of data always include labels for the

Figure 5.2 An actual example of student work graphing simulated data.

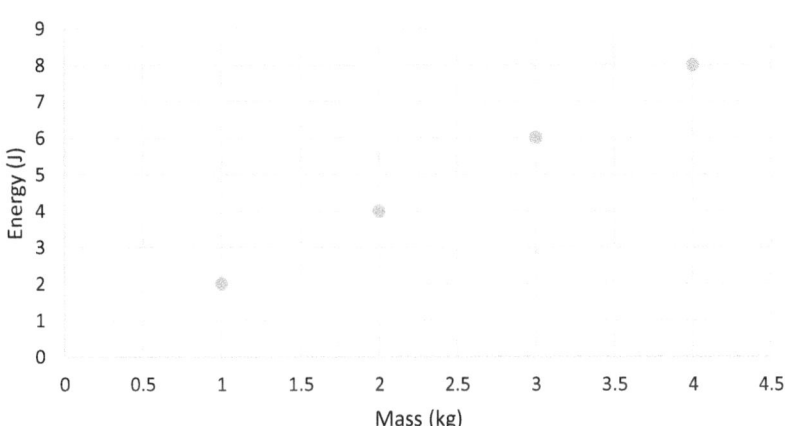

axes including units. In this particular example, a scatter plot (as opposed to a bar chart) is the most appropriate, as well, since we are trying to recognize patterns. Good modeling will always include these characteristics so that students can develop skill at graphing data. The skill is required in order for students to progress to obtaining the ability to interpret the graph.

In Part II of the activity, we begin the process of teaching students how to recognize patterns in data beyond simple increase/decrease relationships. Specifically, when students interpret the mass/energy relationship, they see a simple proportional relationship. In class, you can also highlight the shape of the curve such a relationship exhibits in a graphical display (a straight line) so that they will easily be able to recognize it in the future.

The relationship between the speed and kinetic energy is less obvious. The activity leads students to recognizing the pattern through a series of questions:

- If the speed doubles, by how much does the kinetic energy go up?
- If the speed triples, by how much does the kinetic energy go up?

Working in teams, your students will discover from the graphical display and the raw data that the kinetic energy increases by 4 and then by 9 and then again by 16. Some students will recognize this as a square relationship, where the kinetic energy is equal to the square of the speed, or more simply the speed times the speed. Other students and/or groups will require more coaching to arrive at this pattern. The square relationship arises frequently in physical science, so as students develop, they will encounter this pattern more and more, until it becomes more easily recognized.

When you first start working with your students on quantitatively recognizing patterns in data, then I recommend starting with simulated data as opposed to real data obtained by the student. With simulated data like that seen in Activity 5.2, you can control what the data look like, so you can make the relationship easier for the student to recognize with less intervention. Then, you can tie that relationship to a specific curve shape on a graph that students can more easily recognize in the future. In future lessons, students will have more practice with recognizing similar patterns and will be able to work with more complex and less clear datasets.

Using Mathematics and Computational Thinking

The curves underlying graphical displays like those shown in Figure 5.2 are a type of mathematical representation students can use to make predictions. In Part II, when the student is extrapolating the given data to determine the kinetic energy for mass and speed outside of the supplied data, they are using mathematical thinking. As mentioned above, the act of graphing the data is a skill. However, being able to look at the graph and determine a pattern and then use that pattern to make a prediction is an ability that requires significant intervention to develop.

Table 5.5 shows the generic NGSS evidence statements for the science practice of mathematical thinking. The NGSS expects students to be able to identify the characteristics of a simple mathematical representation and apply the representation to a physical system to identify how it corresponds to physical observations. They also must use the mathematical representation to identify patterns and make predictions based on changing parameters.

In Activity 5.2, we have students identify how energy is affected by changes in physical characteristics of the wagon. Specifically, they can identify that the energy increases as mass and speed increase. For mass, they can quickly identify a linear increase using the mathematical representation of the graph. For the speed, they can identify a non-linear relationship, where the energy makes bigger increases for each interval that the speed increases. By looking at the raw data, they should also be able to identify the pattern with more precision, by recognizing that the kinetic energy is equal to the speed times the speed.

Notice that this final recognition can be facilitated by your choice of data. I intentionally designed the data to make this relationship more obvious. In future lessons, we would either use messier real data, or I would begin to simulate data where the relationship was less obvious. In these future lessons, the student now has to know to look for a pattern and have enough experience to know what types of relationships to look for.

When the student determines the pattern in the data, they now have a model on which to base a prediction. For the example of changes in mass, the student can now predict that increasing the mass by one more kilogram will result in an energy that goes up by 2 Joules. Similarly, they will be able to predict that a speed of 5 meters per second will result in an energy of 5 times 5 Joules (25 J).

TABLE 5.5 EVIDENCE STATEMENTS FOR USING MATHEMATICAL THINKING. ADAPTED FROM NGSS LEAD STATES (2013B).

	The student
1	Identifies the characteristics of a simple mathematical representation
2	Applies the mathematical representation to a physical system to identify how the model characteristics correspond to physical observations
3	Uses the mathematical representation to identify patterns
4	Uses the mathematical representation to make predictions based on changing parameters

Pattern recognition and mathematical thinking are possibly the more difficult science abilities to teach and learn. Comparatively, it is relatively easy to teach a student how to graph data. This is one of the reasons I spent a great number of words discussing the difference between skills and abilities in Chapter 1. If not careful, science teaching can have a tendency to treat the act of graphing data similarly to the ability to understand the data. I have observed numerous classes where the graphing skill is modeled exquisitely and students become extremely proficient at graphing data. However, the interpretation of the data is left implied. Significant time is spent on graphing, with little to no time spent on learning how to interpret. Unfortunately, interpretation requires more practice, more explicit instruction, and more reflection by the student to master.

Let us now look at an example of an assessment of mathematical thinking that could be used formatively in a think-pair-share format, or possibly as a summative assessment. Example 5.2 shows a simple multiple-choice assessment designed by the Stanford NGSS Assessment Project for the following NGSS performance expectation (Dozier, 2017; NGSS Lead States, 2013b):

MS-PS4–1. Use mathematical representations to describe a simple model for waves that includes how the amplitude of a wave is related to the energy in a wave.

Example 5.2 Assessment for mathematical thinking with energy and waves

Figure 5.3 shows the relationship between the amount of energy transferred by an ocean wave and its amplitude.

A company is deciding where to build a plant to generate electricity from ocean wave energy. Individual waves at any location vary in size, so the company measured waves at two locations and calculated the average wave amplitude, shown in the table below.

(Continued)

Example 5.2 (Continued)

Figure 5.3 Transferred energy vs. wave amplitude.

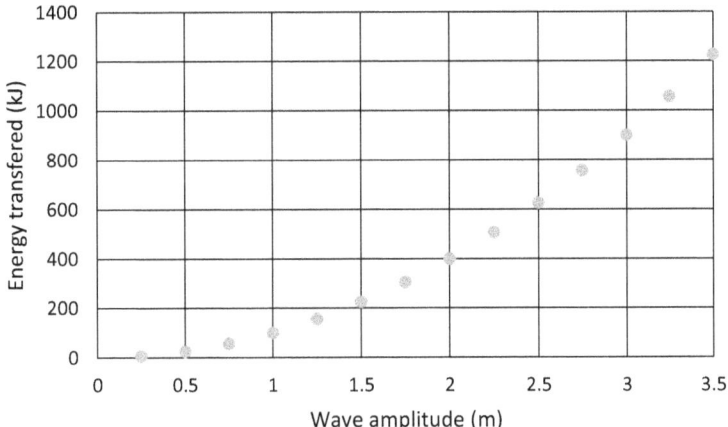

Location	Wave Amplitude	Energy Transferred
A	2 meters	500 kJ
B	4 meters	???

1. Use the graph and the table above to estimate the amount of energy transferred at location B.

    A. 300 kJ
    B. 400 kJ
    C. 800 kJ
    D. 1,600 kJ
    E. 3,200 kJ

2. Using the data above, describe the difference between the amplitude of an average wave in each location.
    Compared to location A, an average wave in location B...

    A. Is taller from the bottom to the top of the wave
    B. Has less energy
    C. Has more distance between it and the next wave
    D. Has less distance between it and the next wave

(Continued)

> **Example 5.2 (Continued)**
>
> 3. How does the energy transferred by a wave change when the energy is doubled?
>
>   The energy transferred . . .
>
>   A. Decreases slightly
>   B. Increases slightly
>   C. Doubles
>   D. More than doubles
>
> Source: Adapted from Dozier (2017).

Designed and validated by Ph.D. student Sara Dozier, this short and simple assessment examines the student's ability to go through a similar process as that in Activity 5.2, only this time in the context of energy and waves.

Data for the relationship between the wave amplitude and the amount of energy transferred is provided in a graphical form. The first question asks the student to use the graph to estimate the energy for a wave amplitude that is not explicitly provided for in the data. To accomplish this, the student must identify the characteristics of the energy/amplitude relationship from the graph: The energy goes up more and more with each interval increase in amplitude. The student then must identify the pattern explicitly (again, a square relationship) in order to make a prediction about what the energy would be for an amplitude of 4 meters.

In the first question, it is possible for the student to determine a correct answer with no content knowledge on waves. The axes could read "banana" and "orange," and the student could still recognize the pattern in the data. The second question assesses the combination of the student's content knowledge and ability to interpret the graph. In particular, to answer correctly, the student must identify the amplitude as the bottom-to-top distance and distinguish it from the frequency. Furthermore, the student must recognize from the data that the wave amplitude is greater at location B.

The last question in the assessment once again checks the student's ability to identify the pattern. Rather than simply extrapolate to 4 meters, students are given a more generic question concerning a doubling of the amplitude.

TABLE 5.6 SAMPLE CHECKLIST FOR THE APPRENTICESHIP-BASED ACTIVITY ON ENERGY AND THE ASSOCIATED ASSESSMENT.

Checklist	Description
Identify the practice and content	The science practices are explicitly identified in the activity. The assessment is based on the evidence statements for the appropriate science practice.
Identify how the student will construct knowledge	The learning progression is clearly laid out. Simulated data are used to provide an easy first experience with data interpretation and mathematical thinking, with the follow-up work requiring more sophisticated and general practice. Students discover from the data the relationship between energy and mass/speed. They are not told the relationship.
Define the community the student will work within	Students work within teams on the activity, negotiating their approach to the questions.
Define the explicit instruction to be given	The activity makes mathematical thinking explicit, requiring the student to find patterns in the data. It is clear that the explicit focus is on pattern recognition within the context of energy.
Identify how you will encourage reflection	To make predictions, students must reflect on the pattern they think they have determined. Furthermore, the same ability is required in a different context for the assessment, inviting the student to reflect on the cross-cutting nature of the practice.
Define how the activity will be made to count	Students are directly assessed on the use of the science practice within the context of the content. It is made clear that future tests will be similar to the formative assessment.

Finally, let's quickly check how a class session using Activity 5.2 and the assessment in Example 5.2 fulfills all of the requirements of the checklist for apprenticeship-based activities we developed in Chapter 2. Table 5.6 shows the checklist for this activity and assessment, where I have outlined how the combination is explicit, reflective, and made to count.

Summary

In this chapter, I have shown examples of how to teach content through the practices of analyzing and interpreting data, using mathematical thinking, and constructing explanations. Specifically, we looked at examples in the context of energy, which is a type of concept termed "theoretical." Students do not have access to directly observable exemplars when working with theoretical concepts. I chose to highlight such a concept in this chapter, because the pedagogical approach to theoretical concepts is similar to the pedagogical approach necessary for the more creative abilities such as pattern recognition necessary to the practices in this dimension.

The following is a brief summary of the main points:

- The goal of science is to provide explanations.
- Interpreting the results of investigations is the sense-making step in science.
- Fundamentally, there are three types of concepts:
    ◇ Concrete: having directly observable exemplars
    ◇ Hypothetical: having observable exemplars, but on scales outside of everyday experiences
    ◇ Theoretical: having no directly observable exemplars
- Teaching theoretical concepts requires you to
    ◇ build off students' existing ideas, and/or
    ◇ begin with more concrete manifestations of the concept.
- Teaching threshold concepts such as pattern recognition require a similar pedagogical approach.

References

Coletta, V. P., & Phillips, J. A. (2005). Interpreting FCI scores: Normalized gain, preinstruction scores, and scientific reasoning ability. *American Journal of Physics, 73,* 1172.

Dozier, S. (2017). *Energy and Ocean Waves.* Retrieved from Stanford NGSS Assessment Project: http://web.stanford.edu/group/ngss_assessment/cgi-bin/snapgse/

Lawson, A. E., Alkhoury, S., Benford, R., Clark, B., & Falconer, K. (2000). What kinds of scientific concepts exist? Concept construction and intellectual development in college biology. *Journal of Research in Science Teaching, 37,* 996.

Lawson, A. E., Clark, B., Cramer-Meldrum, E., Falconer, K. A., Sequist, J., & Kwon, Y. (2000). Development of scientific reasoning in college biology: Do two levels of general hypothesis-testing skills exist? *Journal of Research in Science Teaching, 37,* 81.

Moore, J. C. (2017). Classroom-based science apprenticeships: Preparing future physics teachers to teach science practice. In E. McLoughlin &

P. van Kampen (Eds.), *Groupe International de Recherche sur l'Enseignement de la Physique 2017*. Dublin, Ireland: GIREP.

Moore, J. C., & Rubbo, L. J. (2012). Scientific reasoning abilities of nonscience majors in physics-based courses. *Physical Review Special Topics—Physics Education Research, 8*, 010106.

Moore, J. C., & Slisko, J. (2017). Dynamic Visualizations of Multi-Body Physics Problems and Scientic Reasoning: A Threshold to Understanding. In T. Greczylo & E. Debowska (Eds.), *Key Competences in Physics Teaching and Learning*. New York, NY: Springer.

National Research Council. (2012). *A Framework for K–12 Science Education: Practices, Crosscutting Concepts, and Core Ideas*. Washington, DC: The National Academies Press.

NGSS Lead States. (2013a). APPENDIX E—Progressions Within the Next Generation Science Standards. In N. L. States (Ed.), *Next Generation Science Standards: For States, by States*. Washington, DC: The National Academies Press.

NGSS Lead States. (2013b). *Next Generation Science Standards: For States, by States*. Washington, DC: The National Academies Press.

6

Communicating Science and Building Communities of Practice

"I believe in evidence. I believe in observation, measurement, and reasoning, confirmed by independent observers. I'll believe anything, no matter how wild and ridiculous, if there is evidence for it. The wilder and more ridiculous something is, however, the firmer and more solid the evidence will have to be."

—Isaac Asimov (1997)

The final dimension of science practice is communication. Once a scientist has investigated a phenomenon and interpreted the results, he or she then must communicate those results to the scientific community and/or the public. However, science communication goes beyond simply disseminating results. Science-in-action requires constant communication back-and-forth between others in the scientific community. First and foremost, the scientist must be persuasive to other scientists. Evidence and reason are the coins of the realm, forming the foundation of persuasive arguments. The scientist must also be able to evaluate the results and arguments of others. In particular, they evaluate the relative value of evidence that they gather from other scientists and compile this evidence into a bigger science "story."

It's common to think of the communication dimension of science practice in the traditional sense, with the scientist literally standing in front of a crowd at a conference or writing a paper. Communicating in front of groups and scientific writing are certainly necessary skills the scientist needs. Note, though, that these are *skills* not abilities, and although necessary, they are not sufficient alone for effective scientific communication. There are great books out there on teaching the specific skills involved in communicating science (Worsley & Mayer, 2007). This chapter will not focus on these skills. Instead, it will instead focus on the science practices of arguing from evidence, and obtaining and evaluating information. When writing and speaking skills are built on top of these abilities, then the student of science becomes an *effective* communicator, as opposed to merely a technically proficient communicator.

Specifically, this chapter is focused on getting students to interact with you and each other in the way scientists interact with their colleagues. We will discuss teaching communication practices by building a simulated "community of practice" in your classroom. As a community endeavor, the actual practice of science is socially negotiated, which is one of the underlying principles of situated cognition that we discussed in Chapter 2 (Collins, Brown, & Holum, 1991). For example, the student might question you or her peer: "Why do this in this way? Wouldn't this over here be better?" And the negotiation begins. To convince either you or her groupmate, she must use evidence to support her claim. You and her groupmate can then evaluate the value of the evidence and decide if you are each convinced. We must teach students how to participate in this negotiation. More importantly, you will have to relinquish some of your own control and participate, too.

After discussing communities of practice, we'll look at some simple example activities and assessment rubrics for the science practice dimension of communication. As with the previous chapter, I'll use the checklist for activity development from Chapter 2 as a guide, and I'll also take advantage of the framework for developing assessable curriculum discussed in Chapter 3. There is no singular content focus in this chapter like there was in Chapters 4 and 5. But as you've learned already, the content isn't really the message of this book, anyway.

Communicating Scientific Ideas

The *Framework* states the following about how students should learn to communicate in the science classroom:

> The study of science and engineering should produce a sense of the process of argument necessary for advancing and defending a new idea or an explanation of a phenomenon and the norms for conducting such arguments. In that spirit, students should argue for the explanations they construct, defend their interpretations of the associated data, and advocate for the designs they propose.
> (National Research Council, 2012, p. 73)

In the last chapter, we focused on sense-making, where the student used evidence to build a convincing explanation in their own mind. However, real scientists do not operate on islands, and neither should your students. In the quote above, the *Framework* is describing the necessity for the student to learn to defend their explanations and interpretations. It's not just a matter of mere dissemination, either. We're often wrong or at least misguided! Sometimes, we're missing information that our colleague has that could change our view on a topic. Effective communication is an absolute necessity, because it moves science forward *and* serves as an internal quality check. It also happens in-the-moment as science is being done, rather than only at the conclusion.

Table 6.1 details the science practices outlined by the *Framework* that I have grouped into the communication dimension (National Research Council, 2012). The communication dimension consists of the following two practices:

1. Engaging in argument from evidence
2. Obtaining, evaluating, and communicating information

The scientist gathers evidence in many forms to make an argument for or against a claim. In some cases, the scientist is persuading their colleagues to adopt some approach. In other cases, the scientist is persuading the scientific community that some claim is true or not. It also may be as simple as negotiating with their partner in the laboratory on how long of an interval they should measure, or what other variables might be

TABLE 6.1 SCIENCE PRACTICES WITHIN THE DIMENSION OF COMMUNICATION.

Science Practice	Description
Engage in argument from evidence	The scientist gathers evidence in many forms to make an argument for or against a claim. In some cases, the scientist is persuading their colleagues to adopt some approach. In other cases, the scientist is persuading the scientific community that some claim is true or not. Finally, the scientist must also persuade the non-scientist public. Students must learn how to identify claims, identify and describe evidence, evaluate the value of the evidence, and effectively use reason to build an argument for the claim based on the evidence.
Obtain, evaluate, and communicate information	Not all of the information that scientists obtains come from their own investigations. They must gather, evaluate, and communicate information that comes from a variety of sources. Similarly, the student of science must also gather information about the content, combine that information into a set of evidence, and use the information to tell a "science story."

important. To participate in this type of negotiation, students must learn how to identify claims, identify and describe evidence, evaluate the value of the evidence, and effectively use reason to build an argument for the claim based on the evidence.

Again, from the *Framework*:

> Any education in science and engineering needs to develop students' ability to read and produce domain-specific text. As such, every science or engineering lesson is in part a language lesson, particularly reading and producing the genres of texts that are intrinsic to science and engineering.
>
> (National Research Council, 2012, p. 76)

When this quote talks about a "language lesson," they don't mean a lesson in the context of English, good writing, or public speaking. The type of language being discussed here is the language of science. To speak and write like the scientist. My specific writing style is very different than some of my colleagues, and often times can be in a completely different tongue, but we are all writing in the same language. Our communications start with a claim, presents some evidence, draw from other resources to provide outside evidence, use reasoning to chain all of that evidence to the claim, and solicit the input of our listener/reader. We also know how to pull these elements out of our colleague's communications. It's dialogue.

Since communication in science is more about dialogue than dissemination, we also have to evaluate the communications of others participating in the dialogue. Not all of the information that the scientist obtains comes from their own investigations. In fact, most of the information a scientist gathers in their own work will come from outside sources. As an example, my own research makes up only a tiny fraction of this book. The scientist must gather and evaluate information that comes from a variety of sources. They can then use this information to tell a "science story," where their own work fits into the storyline, or argue for changes in the storyline. Similarly, the student of science must also gather information from others in an attempt to dialogue, combine that information into a set of evidence, and use the information to tell similar stories.

Building a Community of Practice

Let's now discuss the community of science within which we communicate. French sociologist Bruno Latour (1987) observed scientists as they worked and recognized that science is socially constructed. That is to say, the actual practice of science is less a strict method that is objectively applied, and more a process that is socially negotiated. Similarly, psychology and education professor Deanna Kuhn (2004) describes scientific reasoning as a truth-seeking social process that involves the coordination of theory and evidence in a socially negotiated back-and-forth.

This negotiation doesn't happen between the scientist and the non-science public, though. So what the student has typically seen with respect to science communication is different than how scientists communicate with each other. Latour notes that although society has become immersed in science and technology, the actual workings of scientists still remain mysterious to the layperson. The scientists do what they do until they've "made" some new science and/or technology. By the time it hits society, it's become a "black box." Latour (1987) uses the black box as a metaphor for a piece of machinery or even an idea that "runs by itself." Who really knows or cares what's inside a modern cell phone, so long as it's working?

As we've discussed at length throughout the book, traditional science instruction has the tendency to reduce science to black box concepts. In the typical physics classroom, does the student really care how the equations of motion work or where they come from? Or, are they just metaphorically shoving inputs into a black box that spits out an answer? When we treat science as merely the products of that negotiation between scientists, we're really just teaching how to input into black boxes and hope that they still work.

If nothing else, this book has been clear in at least one aspect: Science can only be understood through its practice. Process not products, where the process of science is practiced in a community. Together, the community sets the rules, methods, and standards of discourse. To create new scientists, we must place the young apprentice into the community that practices science so that they can learn science-in-action as opposed to ready-made-science. Learning science-in-action provides them with the abilities necessary to one day be able to make little black boxes of their own. It doesn't work the other way around.

To do this, you will need to build in your classroom what cognitive scientists Lave and Wenger (1991) call a "community of practice" (CoP). So how do we build such a community? Let's first discuss what one is.

Education theorist Etienne Wenger (1998) describes a CoP as any group of people who share a common interest in a domain and a desire to learn from and contribute to the community. Figure 6.1 shows the structural components of a CoP, where domain, community, and practice are the central elements (Wenger, McDermott, & Snyder, 2002). The domain identifies the common area of interest of the group, the community is defined by the interaction between members of the group, and the practice is defined by the focus of the group. Be careful here, because practice in this context is the manner in which the community will develop, share, and maintain its knowledge. In the authentic scientific community, for example, the practice is the set of science practices.

In his book *Communities of Practice*, Wenger (1998) states the following about our participation in such communities and their prevalence:

> We all belong to communities of practice. At home, at work, at school, in our hobbies—we belong to several communities of practice at any given time. And the communities of practice to which we belong change over the course of our lives. In fact, communities of practice are everywhere.
>
> (Wenger, 1998, p. 6)

Figure 6.1 Structural components of a community of practice.

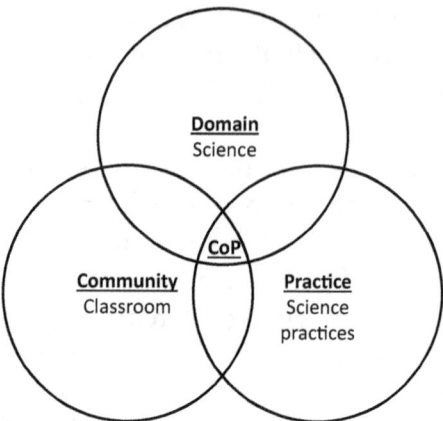

In this interpretation, a CoP is any group of individuals participating in communal activity that creates a shared identity.

As an example, if you're reading this, then you probably teach. You share this with your teacher colleagues. If you meet with your colleagues once a month over beer or wine or ginger ale to talk about your shared experiences in the classroom, your successes and failures, your students, and the activities you've done that you've liked, then you are participating in a CoP. The domain is teaching, the community is your little cohort at the bar, and the practice is those aspects of teaching that work. From this one example of you and your teacher peers, you can also see one other key component: You and your peers are learning, and that learning is happening as a group. Your small group may consist of teachers having varying levels of experience, providing an opportunity for the master teacher to share experience with others. Ultimately, your small cohort supports one another, and ideally, brings the newbie teacher into the fold to help socialize them into the teaching profession.

Let's think about how the apprentice scientist is socialized into the community of scientists. Within the realm of academic science, the budding scientist usually starts their career as a graduate student working in a science lab under the tutelage of a mentor. The laboratory will be populated with a group of people, such as the mentor, post-doctoral researchers, other graduate students, and sometimes undergraduate students. There is a wide range of experience that can be shared among this group. The domain is science, the community is the laboratory, and the practice is the practices of science.

Not all communities are necessarily supportive, as anyone who has had a bad experience in graduate school or jerk colleagues can attest. What makes a strong community? The way in which the participants interact determines the strength of the community (Wenger, McDermott, & Snyder, 2002). If everyone in your teacher group at the bar views the meetings as opportunities for shared learning and interact as peers with a shared goal, then your community is strong. However, if the master teachers see these meetings as mere opportunities to lecture on what the others are doing right and wrong, then the community is significantly less supportive.

This concept of interaction also allows us to tie in our discussion on communication. In this chapter, we have been talking about communication in the interactive sense and language as shared meaning. With respect to communication, individuals in our group of teachers must feel free to engage with the group, and the other members must be willing to listen. With respect to language, there is a mutual understanding about meaning. For example, when one member says "this activity worked," the group has a shared understanding of what "worked" means. Does the group value evidence? If so, what evidence is valued? What does it take to convince the rest of the group that the activity worked? (Note that this shared language in a real CoP can be fluid and negotiated.)

Simulating a Community of Practice in the Classroom

You should now have a good mental model of what a CoP is, but how would you go about building one in your classroom? Ideally, it would be great if you could just throw your students into an authentic research laboratory every day and have them apprentice in what Barab and Hay (2001) refer to as "science at the elbows of experts." Unfortunately, this is impractical. Instead, you will have to build a strong simulated CoP and combine it with the principles of cognitive apprenticeship we discussed in Chapter 2.

As seen in Figure 6.1, the domain and community of your simulated CoP are determined for you. The common area of interest (we hope!) is science, and the community is made up of you and the students in your classroom. In building your CoP you do have the choice of practice. You can build a community that focuses on content, and that develops, shares and maintains its knowledge through listening to you, reading a textbook, and taking notes. The only real community interaction that will happen in this case is when your students get together outside of class to study together. However, if you want a CoP in the classroom, you need to build it based on the practices of science, where students together develop, share, and maintain knowledge by investigating, interpreting, and communicating.

Most of the research on creating CoPs focuses on naturally evolving communities, such as our example of a bar meetup for teachers or the study group trying to decipher your incomprehensible lectures. However, looking through this work, I've identified three interrelated features you will want to implement in your simulated CoP if you want a strong community. These key features are diagramed in Figure 6.2 and are as follows:

- Diversity
- Mutual respect
- Shared language

You can think of these three features as representing a three-legged stool, where if you or your students remove one, then the entire community tumbles and learning from the group becomes significantly more difficult.

If we look at the discussion on what strong CoPs look like in the last section, we see strong communities have varying levels of experience and abilities, sharing and learning from each other. In the classroom, I try to

Figure 6.2 The interrelated features of a strong community.

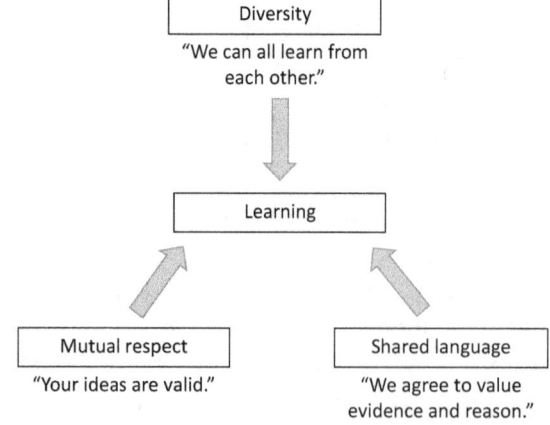

form student groups that have a range of abilities. This means I do my best to identify struggling and thriving students and combine them together into groups. The thriving students are usually those "weird" students like you and me that I talk about in the introduction. The thriving students support the struggling students, and can serve as peer mentors. The struggling students provide a different perspective that the thriving students must confront, which can lead to greater learning on both students' parts. This is the classic example of learning-by-teaching, although don't discount the possibility of the struggling student teaching the thriving student. It happens often in good CoPs.

This mutual learning only happens if all of the students have a mutual respect for one another. For example, the thriving student must resist the urge to lecture or become frustrated, while the struggling student must be willing to share their ideas and thoughts. Mutual respect also means that all students must share in the identity of the group, and be willing participants. The thriving students must be open to questioning, and the struggling students must be willing to question. Furthermore, all ideas within the group need to be seen as valid. We've discussed mental models based on student experiences in Chapter 4. A student's ideas are valid, at least within the frame of view they have constructed. There must be mutual respect for all ideas so that everyone is willing to share. The "winning" idea will be determined by the shared language of the group.

And finally, that shared language in our context means that the group agrees to base decisions on evidence and reason. They will use the science practice dimension of communication to argue like scientists in everything they do. Nobody wins on a vote of "I said so." Even you! Furthermore, the group must agree on the means by which evidence is produced. In our case, this is the science practices.

Notice again that you need all three in order for the group to work effectively as a CoP. Remove one key feature, and the learning community crumbles. For example, if thriving students do not respect the struggling student, they will come to see that student as a burden that slows them down. Furthermore, if the struggling student sees the thriving student as a condescending jerk, then they will get little value out of the community. A homogenous group lacks the diversity of ideas to drive a conversation forward, or worse, struggles to articulate ideas at all. If anyone insists that a decision go their way based on whim, then the community no longer has a shared purpose focused on the process of science. When we say, "my ideas are more valid than yours, yet I offer no evidence," we are signaling our lack of respect for everyone else and negotiation ends.

Practical Components of a Classroom-Based Community of Practice

Let's now look at some practical components of a classroom-based community of practice. Diversity, mutual respect, and shared language are aspects of the community that you need to cultivate, and represent a metaphysical foundation for your CoP. Let's now look at some building blocks you can use to physically build the community. Table 6.2 provides a list of these building blocks and short descriptions of how they can be used.

To be part of a community, students need to work within a community. It's obvious that some level of grouping will be necessary when constructing a CoP. However, if the immediate discussion group is too large, then it creates space for some students to "disappear" within the larger group structure. Within a large group, it becomes easy, specifically for weaker students, to perform the act of physical participation, but not actively contribute mentally to the group's progress, and therefore to their own cognitive development (Apedoe, Ellefson, & Schunn, 2012; Lou et al., 1996). For example, Lohman and Finkelstein (2000) showed that student self-directness increased when working in smaller and medium-sized groups, and decreased in larger groups. However, at some level, the group size becomes too small, such that there is no sense of community or exchange of ideas at all.

In an authentic CoP, the membership is fluid, with members of the community coming and going based on their perception of the continued

TABLE 6.2 THE PRACTICAL COMPONENTS OF A CLASSROOM-BASED COMMUNITY OF PRACTICE THAT YOU CAN IMPLEMENT TOMORROW.

Component	Description
Small groups	Research shows that group sizes of three students is ideal. The groups should be diverse with respect to ability and motivation. Rotate group members every few weeks.
Conferences	Small groups need the opportunity to interact with the rest of the community. Simulated classroom conferences are an excellent way to accomplish this.
Science notebooks	The scientist community uses the scientific notebook as a means to maintain their raw knowledge. The notebook also provides an individual component to the group's work, as well as an assessable item for the individual student.

benefit the community can provide to them. In the classroom setting, you don't have the option of simulating this aspect. Your group is your class of students, and regular classroom order necessitates a more formal structure. With that said, your students do have the option of mentally "coming and going" as they please. To keep them in the game, they need to feel like their contributions matter both to achieving the group goal and to their own learning. Small group sizes between 3 and 4 students appear to accomplish this as best as can be hoped for. Two students is too small, affording less opportunity for legitimate arguments and negotiations. Five or more students becomes too large, where it becomes easy for students to check-out and their mental absence to go unnoticed.

The community of science works in a similar way, where most research happens in small group settings. However, as we've discussed, to drive science forward, these smaller groups interact with the larger community of scientists. In practice, this is done formatively via conferences and similar networking-like events, and summatively via publications. This can be reproduced in the classroom by bringing the smaller groups together to present their ideas to the larger class. I call these larger meetings "conferences."

Let's go back to our discussion about magnets in Chapter 3 for an illustrative example. In one activity, I have student groups plan and conduct an investigation that measures the relative strength of a magnet using only a paperclip and a ruler. The groups generally come up with the same procedure: Measure how far away the paperclip can be placed in front of the magnet right before being pulled into it. The distance is a measure of the strength. In one particular case, I had the students use this method to determine if one pole of a given magnet was stronger than the other. The small work-groups completed the task and then reported their results at conference. Nine groups reported no difference in strength between the north and south poles, and one group reported a difference in strength.

This led to a terrific discussion. First, we had the opportunity to talk about how this is a common occurrence in real science, and is exactly why science is done in a community. Then, we got to talk about the relative value of evidence. We can't discount the one group because nine other groups disagree. They may be right, so we have to look deeper. This led us to an evaluation of all of the groups' methods. It turns out on this occasion, the one group's methods were the most thorough and well documented. They used the same paperclip every time and took care to always face it in the same direction. From this little conference, the larger class was able to determine that the paperclip *was being magnetized*, making the attraction stronger on subsequent measurements. This magnetization was filtered out in the other group's data due to random variation in paperclip direction and less precise measurements.

New learning that I had not planned for happened as a result of that conference. Students not only learned that ferromagnetic materials can be magnetized, but they also learned an important lesson about the process of science. They were getting to see it as the iterative process that it is, instead of the collection of facts they thought it was. To reiterate a point from Chapter 3, if I had built my curriculum based solely on products, this lesson would have never materialized. The conference is an excellent opportunity for you to get feedback that guides your curriculum.

Finally, let's talk about the means by which the scientist documents their experiences in the moment. The scientist community uses the scientific notebook as a means to maintain their raw knowledge. Real science happens over long periods of time, and it's very difficult to remember what happened several weeks ago. A scientist might get good at recognizing patterns in one dataset, but often the patterns that are the most interesting are larger-picture patterns across multiple datasets. It is difficult if not impossible to see these types of patterns without good documentation. In the classroom setting, the notebook also provides an individual component to the group's work, as well as an assessable item for the individual student.

We've looked at a lot of examples of student's writings in their scientific notebooks throughout this book. I'm not going to focus on the individual details of what a notebook should look like, since this can vary across the disciplines. Good note-taking is a skill. I do want to highlight, though, one key aspect that has come up again and again in my classes and that is important to our discussion of communication in science: students *really hate* writing down observations that they don't understand!

Figure 6.3 shows an example from a student's scientific notebook where they are working with electrical switches. In this particular example, the switch is wired in parallel, so that when it is closed, the light goes off. The light goes off when the switch is on! When we first start working with switches, this is absolutely baffling to the students, and most refuse to write down their observation because they can't explain it, or they think it's "wrong." It takes a few more days of observations in this class until

Figure 6.3 An example from a student's scientific notebook where they must document a "weird" observation.

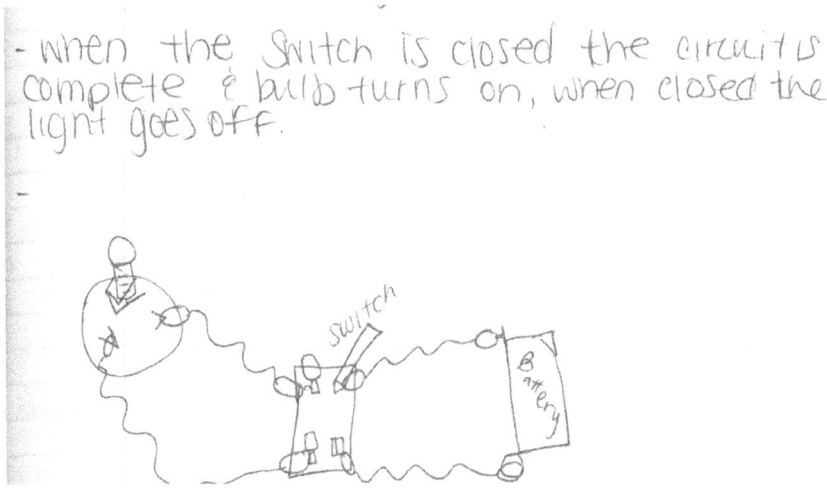

we have enough to find a pattern and come up with an explanation. In this case, it's an explanation for the behavior of current in series and parallel configurations.

When I first started running this activity on switches, I was shocked at how apprehensive students were at simply documenting the observation. This apprehension is ultimately founded in their view that science is a set of "facts" and that the process of learning science involves knowing those facts. The student approach to note-taking is writing down the chunks of facts they need to study to regurgitate on tests. Extraneous stuff gets in the way of "learning." This is not necessarily an invalid approach, since it more than likely served them well in the past.

It takes significant intervention to get students to write down when "weird" stuff happens. However, this is part of communication in science. It's the weird stuff that is the most interesting to the scientific community. As the leader in the classroom, you will need to encourage both the documenting and sharing of weird observations, even if *you* have no clue why they happened. You should be explicit about this, even to the point of setting up weird results yourself. Eventually, students will learn to trust observations they make, and trust that they will eventually be able to determine the why by using the practices of science. If the CoP encourages weird ideas, then really awesome learning happens, and students start to change their views of science to better align with those of the scientist.

Engaging in Argument From Evidence

Let's now bring these pieces together. We're going to build a simple activity that has students working within a community of practice to learn how to argue from evidence. Or in the parlance of the last few sections, they will learn how to communicate using the language of the community. The following NGSS performance expectation for the fifth-grade classroom will be our guide:

5-PS2–1. Support an argument that the gravitational force exerted by Earth on objects is directed down.

Table 6.3 shows the generic NGSS evidence statements for the science practice of arguing from evidence. The NGSS expects students to be able to identify the claim or claims to be supported, identify, and describe the given evidence that supports the claim, evaluate the relative value of that evidence, and use reason to connect the evidence to the claim.

Activity 6.1 uses a chart that makes the expectations within this practice explicit. In this particular activity, students must pull the claim from the short descriptive paragraph and articulate it in their own words. They then must think of multiple pieces of evidence drawn from their own experiences. Finally, they must explicitly state why they think the evidence supports the claim. At the end of the activity, the smaller working groups discuss their evidence and reasoning with the rest of the class. The end result is that the community comes up with potentially dozens of varying arguments for the claim.

TABLE 6.3 EVIDENCE STATEMENTS FOR SUPPORTING AN ARGUMENT FROM EVIDENCE.

	The student
1	Identifies the claim to be supported
2	Identifies and describes the given evidence that supports the claim
3	Evaluates the relative value of the evidence
4	Uses reason to connect the evidence to the claim

Activity 6.1 Gravity and Argument From Evidence

Science Practice: Engage in Argument From Evidence

Jason believes that the gravitational force exerted by the Earth on objects always points directly down. How would you support this argument? With your group, fill in the argument chart. Identify Jason's claim. Then, identify at least three pieces of evidence for that claim. Finally, state the reason you think the evidence supports the claim. After you have completed the argument chart in your small group, we will hold a conference to discuss.

Figure 6.4 Argument chart for structured "argument from evidence" activities.

Claim:	
Evidence:	Reason:
Evidence:	Reason:
Evidence:	Reason:

Table 6.4 shows the checklist for apprenticeship-based activities applied to Activity 6.1. The science practice is explicitly identified in the activity. The students construct their own knowledge, since they determine the evidence and reasoning. They discuss their evidence statements with the larger class, where the community decides the value of the evidence and soundness of the reasoning, instead of an authority. This provides practice in negotiating with a community to create new knowledge.

TABLE 6.4 SAMPLE CHECKLIST FOR THE APPRENTICESHIP-BASED ACTIVITY ON ARGUMENT FROM EVIDENCE AND THE ASSOCIATED ASSESSMENT.

Checklist	Description
Identify the practice and content	The science practices are explicitly identified in the activity. The assessment is based on the evidence statements for the appropriate science practice.
Identify how the student will construct knowledge	The student groups are tasked with determining what constitutes evidence for a given claim. They discuss their evidence statements with the larger class, where the community decides the value of the evidence and soundness of the reasoning, instead of an authority.
Define the community the student will work within	Students work within teams on the activity, negotiating their approach to the claim. Then, the smaller teams discuss their ideas with the larger classroom.
Define the explicit instruction to be given	The activity makes argument from evidence explicit.
Identify how you will encourage reflection	Students must reflect on the value of their evidence. They also must reflect on the value of the evidence shared with them by other groups.
Define how the activity will be made to count	Students are directly assessed on the use of the science practice within the context of the content. It is made clear that future tests will be similar to the formative assessment.

The activity makes argument from evidence explicit by using a chart. This argument-from-evidence chart can be used in other contexts, too. The activity is reflective because it forces students to think about their own thinking and the thinking of their peers. A student is less likely to blindly accept evidence and reasoning from a peer as opposed to you. And finally, because it is context-independent, the argument-from-evidence chart can be used as an assessment, with its structure reproduced in future assessments. The actual practice of arguing from evidence is being made to count.

Let's think about the activity in terms of its ability to help build community. First, we have the practical building blocks with small groups negotiating their way to consensus, followed by a larger community conference that can facilitate expanded discussion. The participants in the simulated CoP are learning to communicate (the shared language) in a way similar to that used in an authentic scientific CoP. The stakes here are low, meaning that the student feels little pressure to "learn" some fact. This makes it more likely that the practice of mutual respect will flourish within the groups. And finally, there are many possibilities for evidence, which allows a diversity of ideas to be shared and ultimately accepted by the community.

Obtaining, Evaluating, and Communicating Scientific Information

Notice in the last activity, the students were also implicitly obtaining and evaluating information from their peers. When they looked at the evidence and reasoning their peer was attempting to use to support the claim, they had to evaluate in their own mind whether it made sense to them. Scientists have to evaluate the communications of others to participate in the dialogue of science.

This brings us to our final science practice: obtaining, evaluating, and communicating information. Table 6.5 shows the generic NGSS evidence statements for this science practice. The NGSS expects students to be able to gather information from a variety of different types of sources. The types of sources will be context depended. Once gathered, the student then must be able to extract from the information a claim or in some cases competing claims about a phenomenon. Within the information should be some evidence that is used to support the claim. The student needs to be able to recognize this evidence. Finally, the student combines all of the information from all sources to evaluate the total evidence with respect to the claim.

The following are two examples of NGSS performance expectations for this practice:

MS-PS4–3. Integrate qualitative scientific and technical information to support the claim that digitized signals are a more reliable way to encode and transmit information than analog signals.

4-ESS3–1. Obtain and combine information to describe that energy and fuels are derived from natural resources and their uses affect the environment.

TABLE 6.5 EVIDENCE STATEMENTS FOR OBTAINING AND EVALUATING INFORMATION.

	The student
1	Gathers information from a variety of different types of sources
2	Extracts from the information a claim or competing claims about a phenomenon
3	Extracts from the information evidence that is used to support the claim
4	Combines the information to evaluate the total evidence with respect to the claim

In the first example, middle school students are looking for sources of information that make the claim that digitized signals are more reliable. In the second example, elementary school students are looking for sources of information that claim energy is derived from natural resources. In both cases, they must find information, extract from the information the claim that the author is making, the evidence that the author is using, and the reasoning chain that the author uses to tie the evidence to the claim. They compile the resources and evaluate the totality of the evidence.

How might we use this in the classroom? The specifics depend on whether we are at the level of modeling, coaching, or scaffolding. However, one example would be to provide your students with several pieces of information, whether articles, graphs, videos, or some combination. From each piece of information, have them fill out an argument-from-evidence chart similar to the one used in Activity 6.1. This would allow you to develop and then assess the student's ability to evaluate the information obtained.

You can also send your student out to search for information. First, you would model how this is done for your discipline. Then, allow the student access to the tools to search for information on the subject matter. Now, they can evaluate that information, compile it together, and present it at a class conference. The focus, of course, being on the claims and evidence being made by the authors, and whether or not the reasoning is valid.

After enough work on this practice, I like to lead my students to some of the less scientific corners of the internet. Specifically, I might show them a series of articles making claims about how the U.S. government faked the moon landing, or that shape-shifting lizard people exist among us, or that aliens built the pyramids. I have the students go through this information, identify the claim, identify the evidence that the author uses (or identify whether any evidence is produced at all), and then evaluate that evidence with respect to the claim and the author's chain of reasoning. I might give a different article to each group, and then have them meet and discuss in a conference. You better believe the conversation gets interesting!

Let's look at how to build a rubric to assess these types of activities. Example 6.1 shows a sample rubric for obtaining and evaluating information. The top level of the rubric is generic and is based on pieces of the NGSS evidence statements for each practice. The individual criterions are specific to the content we have the student investigating and interpreting.

Example 6.1 Rubric for assessment of obtaining and evaluating information

Obtains information

	Unsatisfactory	Needs Improvement	Satisfactory
Obtains information from a variety of sources	The student does not obtain any information.	The student obtains information from only one source.	The student obtains information from at least two sources.
Identifies the claim being made in each source	The student does not identify any claims.	The student attempts to identify claims, but does not identify the claims correctly.	The student correctly identifies the claims being made in the information.
Identifies the evidence being used to support the claims	The student does not identify evidence.	The student attempts to identify evidence, but does not identify the evidence correctly.	The student correctly identifies the evidence used in the information to support the claims.

Evaluates information

	Unsatisfactory	Needs Improvement	Satisfactory
Identifies the reasoning chain used in the information to link the evidence to the claim	The student does not identify reasoning.	The student attempts to identify reasoning, but does so incorrectly.	The student correctly identifies the reasoning chain.
Evaluates the value of the evidence and reasoning	The student does not evaluate the value of the evidence and reasoning.	The student attempts to evaluate the value, but is unclear.	The student evaluates the evidence and reasoning, and makes a statement on the weight they place on the information based on this evaluation.

(Continued)

Example 6.1 (Continued)

	Unsatisfactory	Needs Improvement	Satisfactory
Combines the information to tell a story	The student does not combine the information.	The student attempts to combine the information, but does not tell a clear OR consistent story about the information.	The student combines the information with all evidence and reasoning to tell a story about the claim, whether supportive or unsupportive.

Summary

In this chapter, I have shown examples of how to teach content through the practices of engaging in argument from evidence, and obtaining, evaluating, and communicating information. Specifically, this chapter has focused on teaching the student how to communicate within the community of science. To this end, we discussed how to build a community of practice in the classroom, where students work in small teams, share their team's ideas in classroom conferences, and document their developed knowledge in science notebooks. The importance of cultivating diversity of ideas, mutual respect, and shared language was discussed. Finally, we looked at several specific examples of activities that foster scientific communication in-action within the classroom environment.

The following is a brief summary of the main points:

- Scientists communicate with each other in a dialogue with a shared respect for evidence.
- Science is socially constructed and built from a negotiation between scientists.
- When students learn to communicate like scientists, they can start to move away from a "black box" view of science and how it's constructed.
- Communities of practice are built around shared interests (domain), shared identity (community), and shared language (practice).
- A simulated community of practice in the classroom must demonstrate all of the following:

- ◇ Diversity of ideas
- ◇ Mutual respect
- ◇ Shared language

♦ The practical building blocks of a simulated community of practice in the classroom are as follows:

- ◇ Small groups
- ◇ Conferences
- ◇ Science notebooks

♦ Using a chart to diagram claims, evidence, and reason makes the practice of argument from evidence explicit.

♦ Students need to learn how to evaluate the arguments of others.

References

Apedoe, X. S., Ellefson, M. R., & Schunn, C. D. (2012). Learning together while designing: Does group size make a difference? *Journal of Science Education and Technology*, 21(1), 83–94.

Asimov, I. (1997). *The Roving Mind*. Amherst, NY: Prometheus Books.

Barab, S., & Hay, K. (2001). Doing science at the elbows of experts: Issues related to the science apprenticeship camp. *Journal of Research in Science Teaching*, 38(1), 70–102.

Collins, A., Brown, J., & Holum, A. (1991). Cognitive apprenticeship: Making thinking visible. *American Educator*, 6, 38–46.

Kuhn, D. (2004). What is scientific thinking and how does it develop? In U. Goswami (Ed.), *Blackwell Handbook of Childhood Cognitive Development*. Malden, MA: Wiley-Blackwell.

Latour, B. (1987). *Science in Action: How to Follow Scientists and Engineers Through Society*. Milton Keynes, UK: Open University Press.

Lave, J., & Wenger, E. (1991). *Situated Learning: Legitimate Peripheral Participation*. New York: Cambridge University Press.

Lohman, M. C., & Finkelstein, M. (2000). Designing groups in problem-based learning to promote problem-solving skill and self-directedness. *Instructional Science*, 28(4), 291–307.

Lou, Y., Abrami, P. C., Spence, J. C., Poulsen, C., Chambers, B., & d'Apollonia, S. (1996). Within-class grouping: A meta-analysis. *Review of Educational Research*, 66, 423–458.

National Research Council. (2012). *A Framework for K–12 Science Education: Practices, Crosscutting Concepts, and Core Ideas*. Washington, DC: The National Academies Press.

Wenger, E. (1998). *Communities of Practice: Learning, Meaning, and Identity*. Cambridge: Cambridge University Press.

Wenger, E., McDermott, R., & Snyder, W. M. (2002). *Cultivating Communities of Practice*. New York, NY: Harvard Business Press.

Worsley, D., & Mayer, B. (2007). *The Art of Science Writing*. New York, NY: Teachers & Writers Collaborative.

Part III
Putting It All Together

7

Capstones to Learning and Going Beyond the NGSS

"A great discovery solves a great problem, but there is a grain of discovery in the solution of any problem. Your problem may be modest, but if it challenges your curiosity and brings into play your inventive faculties, and if you solve it by your own means, you may experience the tension and enjoy the triumph of discovery."
—George Pólya (2004, p. i)

Throughout this book, we've talked about engaging students in apprenticeship activities and slowly removing the training wheels. We've discussed how to use cognitive apprenticeship as a framework to design and implement lessons that teach students how to use the practices of scientists to discover for themselves great science content. In previous chapters, we discussed going beyond the narrow Next Generation Science Standards (NGSS) performance expectations and coaching students through the entire science cycle as they learn new content. Now, it's time to put all the pieces together and design a capstone experience that places students as leaders in the discovery process, where they use that previous learning to answer authentic new questions about the world. The final component of cognitive apprenticeship is exploration. In exploration, students investigate new methods, strategies, and test new hypotheses by exploring the problem.

Students set their own goals and develop their own testing strategies, all of which fosters independent learning.

This chapter is about *authentic* explorations that students complete with little guidance and that tie together the entire science cycle from observations, to models, to testing experiments, to analysis, and finally to communication. Explorations come at the end of learning units, because content understanding is required for successful student exploration within the domain. Therefore, I consider these types of activities as excellent capstones to learning. They force reflection on material previously learned, as well as focused application of the science practices. These types of activities expand on the narrow NGSS student performance expectations, preparing students for the independent practice of science. In this final chapter and through these capstone experiences, we get to see before our eyes the creation of a new scientist!

Specifically, I'm going to describe a capstone experience on electric circuits that is designed to take students through the entire science cycle in less than 2 hours of instructional time. (This chapter is an expansion of an article that I wrote for *The Physics Teacher*, to which you can find reference in the references section at the end of the chapter [Moore & Rubbo, 2016].) Students will utilize all eight of the science practices we have focused on in this book to discover the answer to one research question. Furthermore, this particular activity will force students to reflect on the tentative nature of science, pushing them to develop those expert-like views we talked about in Chapter 1. Finally, they will answer a research question using only the evidence they can provide, because even though there is a "correct" answer, we will never tell them what it is. In science, we often can't open the black box to peek inside, and we'll look at an activity that forces students to confront this reality.

What Do We Want to Accomplish With a Capstone?

Real scientists practice science as an integrated system of practices, not as individual, isolated practices to be applied a little here and some over there. In the past, standards separated Disciplinary Core Ideas (DCIs) from practices, leading to the practical effect of each dimension being taught and assessed individually. This has changed with the *Framework* and the NGSS, but we could similarly fall into the trap of assuming that since performance expectations are broken up into individual practices on content, there is no need to see students using the entire system of science to answer a question. A scientist can never be created unless we let them loose on a problem, free to use the arsenal or practices as they see fit.

You need to be careful not to isolate the practices, since they are pieces of a puzzle, that when put together, show the full picture of science. We want students to see the entire picture. We talked about this in previous chapters, but in that case, I wanted you to see and appreciate how the different practices are intertwined, and how you can and should go beyond the explicit performance expectations as students are learning new content. In this chapter, we'll talk about using capstones on learning units that bring all of the practices together to accomplish one scientific goal on a topic already learned. We'll also use the capstone to begin developing more expert-like views about science in areas that can be tricky to pull off during regular learning units.

In my teaching, I have three fundamental goals: (1) I want students to learn science content, (2) by learning how to practice science, and (3) I want to move students toward more expert-like views about science. Basically, I want students to be science literate, science competent, and to think like a scientist. Therefore, a good capstone experience will:

1. Reinforce previously learned material
2. Have students use practices in new ways
3. Promote expert-like views about science

We've spent a lot of chapters talking about teaching through practice already, but what about shifting student views? Let's review the student and expert views about the structure, methodology, and validity of science. Table 7.1 shows both the student and expert views across these dimensions,

TABLE 7.1 TAXONOMY OF STUDENT AND EXPERT VIEWS ABOUT SCIENCE (HESTENES & HALLOUN, 1998).

Dimension	How Students View Science	How Experts View Science
Structure	Science is a loose collection of directly perceived facts.	Science is a coherent body of knowledge about patterns in nature.
Methodology	The methods of science are specific to the discipline.	The methods of science are cross-cutting.
Validity	Scientific knowledge is exact, absolute, and final.	Scientific knowledge is tentative and refutable.

as we have discussed previously in Chapter 1 (Hestenes & Halloun, 1998). To accomplish the third item on our list above, we will want to design an experience that explicitly highlights at least one of the expert-like views. For the example in this chapter, we will be highlighting the view of science as tentative and refutable. Specifically, students will learn that science can be messy and that our simple explanations of reality often require expansion and/or revision based on new evidence.

There is an important reason why I'm waiting until the capstone to begin tackling this subject. This view of science can be *cognitively jarring* for students. First, it goes against their current understanding of science. Second, it fundamentally means that there really isn't a "right" answer beyond what they can convince others of through evidence. This need to "know" the "correct" answer is strong, particularly with your best students. In many cases, they have been conditioned to seek correct answers so that they can repeat them on tests, where they receive rewards for doing well. "Sure. Sure. These practices are fun and important and all, but I need to know what to write on the exam! What's the right answer?"

For this reason, when I design capstones, I choose a research question that goes beyond the content knowledge spelled out in the DCIs. We have to be careful not to lose the student. As an example, in Chapter 3, we discussed the practice-based learning cycle for magnets and magnetic fields. There is very specific content we want the student to learn as they practice science in the magnet domain. We brought almost all of the practices to bear in the teaching of magnet content. However, we never forced the student to contemplate the tentative nature of science. We never "learned" something, and then turned around and said: "Ah ha! What we just learned is actually not quite complete. Here's more!" But science actually is this way. As the student progresses through the grades, they will learn that their previous learning was tentative and that their models need to grow to better explain the world. We need to prepare them for that; however, if we do it too fast, students might feel like they aren't learning *anything*.

If we want to create a scientist instead of a living encyclopedia, then we need to go ahead and jar that student. This is where the capstone can shine, because we can force students to confront this view in a less threatening manner. Why? Because in the capstone, the student will be answering some very specific question, and ideally, one that doesn't seem like a "science fact" like magnetic fields. In the example that follows, I had students use the science process to determine how a group of light bulbs is wired, with the wiring hidden inside of a black box. It's a real, authentic research question. But they know that inside the box, there could be many different configurations and their fundamental understanding of circuits itself is not being challenged. See the difference?

Black Box Circuits: An Authentic Science Exploration

Figure 7.1 shows a plastic project box with three miniature light bulbs protruding from holes on the top. Two wires exit the box from the side. Inside the box, the bulbs are wired in one of four possible configurations. These configurations are as follows:

A. All three bulbs in series
B. All three bulbs in parallel
C. One bulb in parallel with two bulbs in series
D. One bulb in series with two bulbs in parallel

The research question for students is the following: What is the circuit configuration, and how can it be determined without opening the box? In this classroom activity, we guide the students through the process of using models to make predictions, designing experiments that can distinguish between two models that make similar predictions, and revising models based on new information. Throughout the entire process, the practices are being reinforced, with students also having to argue from evidence, and constantly communicate with their scientific community in the

Figure 7.1 Black project box with three exposed light bulbs connected in a hidden configuration. Two wires protrude from the side.

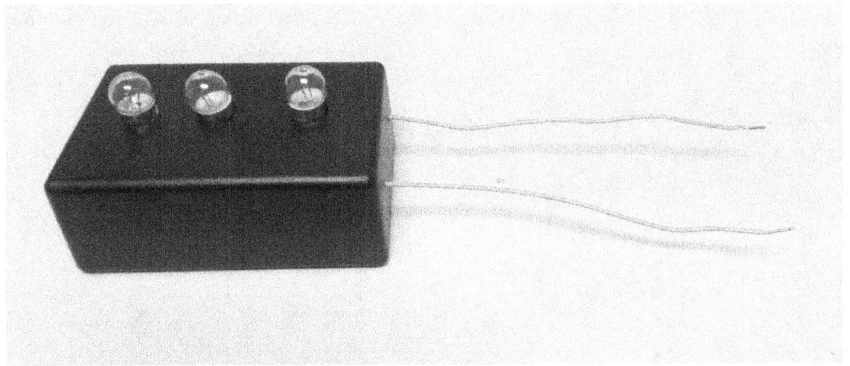

classroom. Finally, we'll begin the process of cementing expert-like views of science through reflection and model revision.

Expanding on Previous Learning: Using and Testing Models

We begin this specific capstone activity by having students determine the four possible configurations of light bulb wiring, which reinforces previous learning on circuits. The student groups are given a light bulb box and no other equipment. They can inspect the box, but they can't make any measurements. We have the students work in teams to describe schematically all of the possible configurations in the box and make predictions concerning relative bulb brightness for each configuration if they were to attach a battery across the two wires.

Figure 7.2 shows an excerpt of a student notebook where all four possible configurations described above can be seen. Figure 7.3 shows an excerpt from another student notebook where the student can be seen making a prediction about the relative brightness of the bulbs. I want to remind you that this activity is a capstone experience for a learning unit on electric circuits, so ranking bulb brightness for these four configurations is a learned ability on which we have already spent a considerable amount of time. Because of this, our students generally have little difficulty constructing these configurations and ranking bulb brightness. If you would like to know more specifically about teaching circuits in elementary and middle school classrooms, then see the excellent book *Physics by Inquiry* in the references section at the end of this chapter.

In this beginning exercise, we are reinforcing previously learned material. Furthermore, it is also an example of the science practice of developing

Figure 7.2 Excerpt from a student notebook showing the possible circuit configurations within the box.

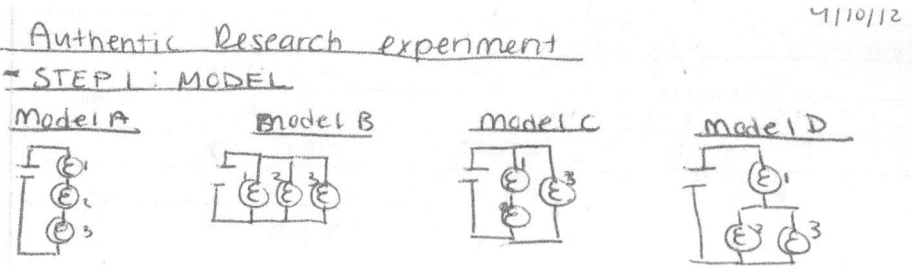

Figure 7.3 Excerpt from a student notebook that demonstrates students making predictions about relative bulb brightness based on the possible circuit configurations.

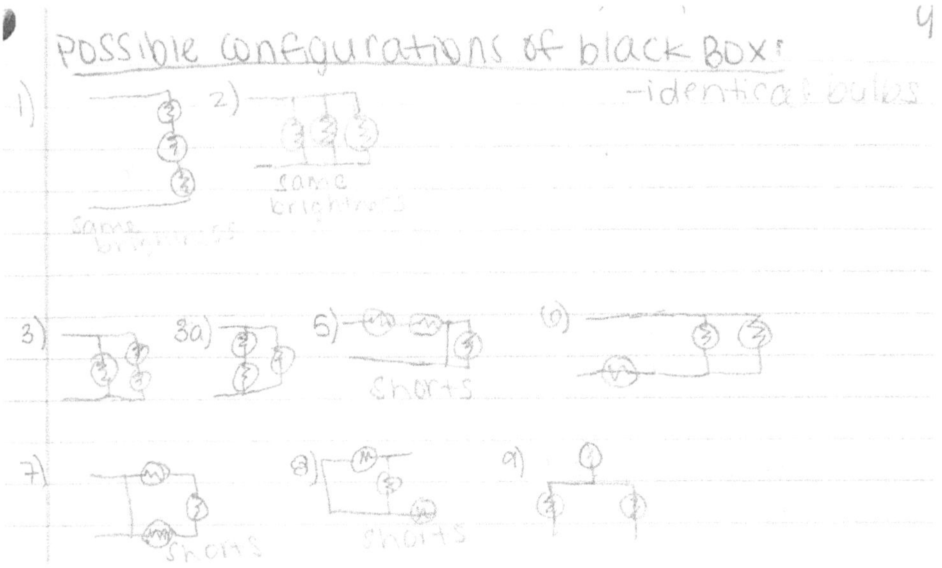

and using models. Essentially, we lead the students to recognize that there are four potential physical models for the system that they are interested in studying. Each of these models results in predictions for the system's behavior when a battery is attached. They can use the four models to make and compare predictions.

If a battery is attached to circuit configurations A and B, all of the bulbs will have the same brightness. For circuit configurations C and D, one bulb will be brighter than the other two bulbs. It is important to highlight that the students do not know how the bulbs are oriented with respect to each other inside the box. This means, for example, that the two outside bulbs could be dim, while the center bulb could be bright. Some students will make the mistake of assuming a physical orientation similar to the schematic orientation within their model, and intervention on this point may be necessary.

Articulation and the Scientific Notebook: Encouraging Reflection In-Action

After all groups have determined possible configurations and brightness predictions, we have students develop explanation-testing experiments that could be used to distinguish between the four configurations. Students are provided the following constraints:

- They are not allowed to remove the bulbs from the boxes.
- We do not provide students with additional equipment until they explicitly ask for it and explain to an instructor or teaching assistant how the equipment will be used.
- We require explicit documentation.

This forces students to engage in predictive model making. Our intention here is to highlight the difference between "explanation-generating" and "explanation-testing" experiments. For the former, students observe and describe phenomena and then analyze data in a search for patterns that can lead to explanations. In the latter, students make predictions based on previously generated explanations and test those explanations. Here, students are applying the concepts and explanations of electric circuits that they have learned throughout the learning unit to make predictive models that they can use to answer a research question, in this case, how the light bulbs are connected.

Many groups initially request only a battery, since they have made predictions already about relative bulb brightness based on attaching a battery to the exposed wires. However, configurations A and B result in the same predictions, as do configurations C and D. When we force students to be explicit about what data will be provided from their test, and what evidence it can provide to answer the research question, more depth of discussion within the groups is usually achieved. As an example, for configurations A and B, some students argue that the bulbs in series will be dimmer than the bulbs in parallel. Sometimes the group will naturally come to the realization that they only have one box and that a comparison across boxes cannot be made. For other groups, explicit instructor intervention is necessary to lead students to this realization. Typically, we lead a whole-class discussion on this point.

This process of forcing the students to think critically about their own thinking is important for the development of strong metacognitive skills in general. It is also an important aspect of the process of science. Specifically, during this phase of the activity, we explicitly coach students in evaluating the *relative value of evidence*. They now must think deeper to devise a test that can distinguish two different models that make similar predictions, and be confident in their results without resorting to unfounded

Figure 7.4 Excerpt from a student notebook that demonstrates students devising experiments whose results can distinguish between two competing configurations that result in similar predictions.

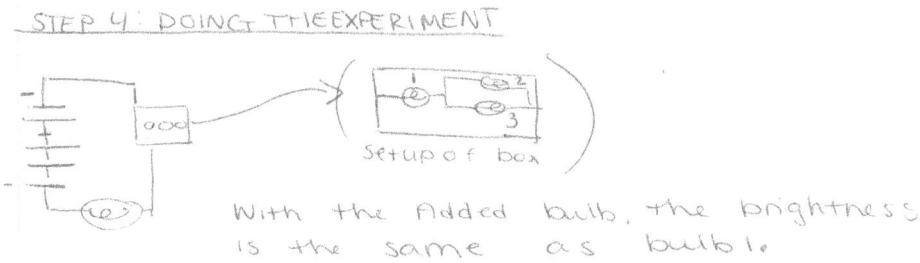

assumptions (such as, these bulbs are exactly like the bulbs we have worked with in the past, so I know how bright they should be).

Figure 7.4 shows an excerpt from a student notebook demonstrating the types of explanation-testing experiments student groups propose to determine which configuration they have. This student describes the experiment as follows:

> Adding a bulb to models C and D will make us identify whether our assumption is correct. In model C, if a bulb is added in series, the added bulb will be the brightest, then 1 = 2 < 3. In model D, if you add the bulb also in series, the new bulb will be the same brightness as bulb 1 which would be brighter than bulbs 2 and 3.

The addition of one bulb in series with the battery and the black box allows the group to distinguish between configurations C and D.

Science Is Tentative: Revising Models to Account for New Evidence

After an instructor or teaching assistant has discussed with a group their proposed explanation-testing experiments, and what the results should be for various options, they are given the requested equipment to perform the experiments. At this point, students realize that something is very different about the light bulbs in the box compared to the light bulbs they have been using throughout the learning unit. Figure 7.5 shows the inside of one of the boxes (not visible to the students), where it can be seen that

Figure 7.5 A photograph of the inside of one of the light bulb boxes. Diodes can be seen to be included in the circuit, which results in a battery-orientation dependence on the bulb behavior.

we have utilized diodes in the configuration, adding a directional component to the problem.

Most groups recognize a dependence on battery orientation very quickly and with little-to-no instructor intervention. Figure 7.6 shows an excerpt from a student notebook where the observations of directionality are documented. As an aside, we would like to mention that getting students to write down "strange" behavior that they cannot initially explain is very difficult, and we work with students on this aspect of science documentation throughout the academic year.

Up until this point in the course, the current model being used by students has had no directional component. In fact, we have explicitly highlighted during previous meetings that from the observations we have made, it does not seem like direction makes any difference at all. In fact, in a previous meeting, we explicitly tested whether battery orientation had any effect on circuit behavior for many types of circuit configurations. We have never discussed diodes, though some students do know what a diode is from some prior knowledge. This is the first experience students have with the directionality of current.

Students must now *revise* their models to include a directional component where bulbs only light for specific battery orientations. An excerpt of a student notebook showing how students decide to model this new phenomenon is shown in Figure 7.7. Interestingly, students arrive at a component schematic similar to an actual diode representation, similar to how the Kindergarten Sun Ray Model of Light in their brains from early childhood is actually a representation similar to the ray model we use in

Figure 7.6 Excerpt from a student notebook showing a student documenting the observations of the directional dependence.

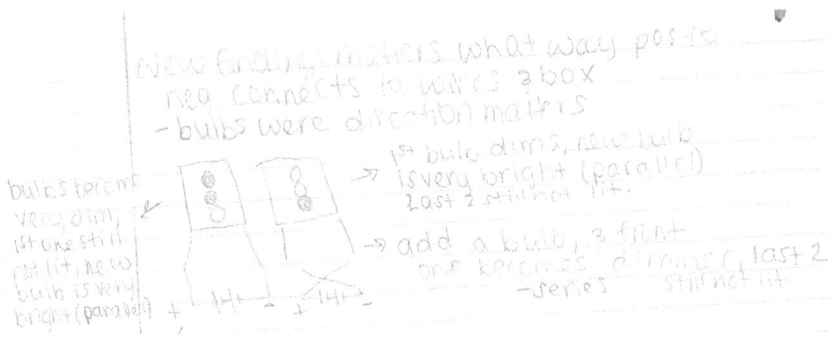

Figure 7.7 Excerpt from a student notebook showing revised circuit configurations based on a new model of light bulbs demonstrating direction dependence.

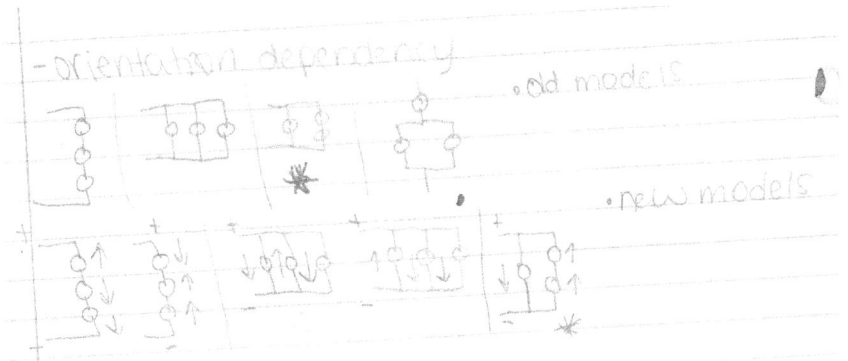

physical science. This "twist" on the experiment exposes students to a new phenomenon that requires them to revise their model by incorporating new observations never previously explored in the coursework.

Reflecting on the Practice of Science

In 6 years of conducting this activity with over 200 students from various backgrounds, we have never had a group that did not ultimately determine the configuration of the bulbs in their box. On a few occasions, boxes have developed defects (such as shorts or open faults), and these defects were correctly identified by the few groups unfortunately given a faulty box.

We also never tell students whether or not they are correct, and we certainly do not grade students based on whether their final conclusion was correct. This activity is about the process of science and not necessarily the accuracy of the student's model. We point out that if they are convinced based on the evidence they have collected, and they can convince others, then that should be good enough. That is, after all, the way real science works. Nature never tells us explicitly whether or not we are right.

Table 7.2 shows the checklist for the activity, explicitly laying out how it is explicit, reflective, and made to count. In particular, this entire activity is designed to mirror the practice of science by actual scientists. We have the student go through all three dimensions of science practice (investigation, interpretation, and communication) in one laboratory period. Students learn the process of making models, developing and conducting testing experiments that can support or falsify models, and confronting ways of distinguishing between two different models that make similar predictions. They also learn that science can be messy and that our simple explanations of reality often require expansion and/or revision based on new evidence.

TABLE 7.2 THE CHECKLIST FOR THE BLACK BOX LIGHT BULB CAPSTONE EXPERIENCE.

Checklist	Activity
Constructs knowledge through practice	A student that demonstrates understanding can use a model for electric circuits to *investigate* the hidden electrical connections between light bulbs. Students must *interpret* data to distinguish between competing models. Finally, students must argue from evidence in the *communication* of their conclusions.
Builds community of practice	The student will work on a small team. Teams will then meet with other teams to hold conferences to discuss their ideas. Each team will present to the entire class during a whole-class conference at the end. The instructor guides students to correctly apply the model and argue from evidence to support conclusions.
Is explicit	Students are explicitly told that they will be using the science practices of "using a model" and "arguing from evidence." During conferences, the instructor will highlight the importance of articulation with the peer group.
Is reflective	Students must reflect on their models, specifically when they find that observed behavior conflicts with their preconceived ideas of how the system should behave. This forces reflection and re-evaluation. The potential for hidden faults in the circuit also forces student reflection on the relative value of evidence.
Is made to count	The student documents the entire experience in their scientific notebook. This notebook is evaluated based on a pre-assigned rubric that focuses on the process of exploration, as opposed to the result.

Let's look back at the expanded model for the scientific method that we developed in Chapter 1. Figure 7.8 shows the science practices and how they are intertwined. In this capstone, the students went through the entire process, starting with asking a question about the configuration of the circuit to communicating their findings to the class. In this particular example, students even got to follow the arrow from testing experiment back to the top of the process after determining their original model was not supported. In conferences, students had to argue from evidence. Finally, at the end of the activity, students had to communicate their result and make their case to their peers.

I actually use this particular exploration capstone near the beginning of my physical science courses for elementary and middle school pre-service teachers, because it is such a great introduction to science process. In particular, the possible configurations are constrained, the ideas generated by the students are predictable, the content is accessible, the stakes are low, and the entire activity can be completed in a single laboratory period. This allows us to build greater sophistication into our process as the semester progresses. It also provides an excellent introduction to the entire science process and the interconnected nature of the practices.

Figure 7.8 A more accurate model of how the scientist practices science.

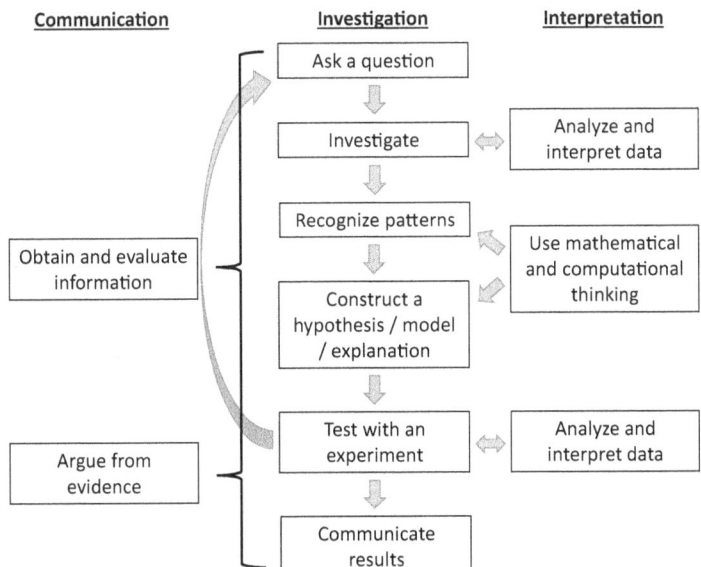

Going Beyond the NGSS

In addition to describing the development of capstone explorations, I also have one other goal for this chapter. I want you to start thinking *beyond* the narrow confines of the NGSS. I decided to use electric circuits as an example in this final chapter exactly because circuits aren't explicitly addressed in the NGSS DCIs or performance expectations. The NGSS should be considered as a set of *minimum* standards. Specifically, for students that we expect could move on from K–12 to pursue further education in the sciences, we would expect a greater depth and breadth of content. This is especially true in secondary science courses, such as physics, where the NGSS DCIs fail to cover some significant and relevant content.

There was actually significant debate about this very issue during the drafting of both the *Framework* and the subsequent NGSS, with the American Association of Physics Teachers stating the following:

> We are concerned that there seem to be almost no standards relating to electric circuits. We recognize that lacuna was inherited from the Framework. However, electrical technology is pervasive in today's world both in everyday home life and cutting-edge technology. Batteries, bulbs, motors, switches and modern high capacity capacitors provide an excellent area of study where students can construct devices and build simple qualitative and quantitative models of the behavior of electric circuits. Activities that emphasize construction, measurement, and modification of circuits could work well at the middle school level and high school level using the engineering practices. Circuits also provide very nice examples of conservation of energy and conservation of electrical charge.
> (American Association of Physics Teachers, 2013, p. 3)

It should be pointed out that the committee that wrote the *Framework* on which the NGSS are based specifically chose to limit the number of DCIs to ensure educators adequately focus on getting "students to engage in scientific investigations and argumentation," rather than a checklist of content (National Research Council, 2012, p. 11). Furthermore, the writers of the NGSS are clear that the performance expectations are not curriculum, and serve as a *minimum* set of standards, stating the following in the executive summary:

> The NGSS are standards, or goals, that reflect what a student should know and be able to do—they do not dictate the manner or methods by which the standards are taught. The performance expectations are written in a way that expresses the concept and skills to be performed but still leaves curricular and instructional decisions to states, districts, school and teachers. The performance expectations do not dictate curriculum; rather, they are coherently developed to allow flexibility in the instruction of the standards.
> (NGSS Lead States, 2013b, p. 2).

Going forward, many states and/or school systems will choose to include performance expectations that go beyond the NGSS. As an example, the science standards in South Carolina are based on the *Framework*; however, performance expectations adopted by the South Carolina Department of Education specifically address electric circuits beginning in the third grade (South Carolina Department of Education, 2014). As a teacher, you need to be prepared to go beyond the NGSS when necessary. In some instances, it is pedagogically necessary, while in others it will be necessary due to state and/or district level demands. Don't let the NGSS hold you back!

Science Has Blurry Borders. Don't Build Fences.

When you first start to reform your teaching by incorporating practice-centric activities, it's probably wise to begin by specifically developing and implementing classroom activities that directly address NGSS performance expectations. However, as you grow more comfortable teaching through practice, you will begin to realize that the practices themselves don't have easily identifiable "borders." An observation experiment leading to a recognizable pattern necessarily becomes a lesson in argument from evidence and explanation construction. Working in a team to develop and use a model often requires abilities at analyzing data and using mathematics. In reality, the practices are intertwined. This was my argument in the previous chapters for why your teaching in one area of content should include most if not all of the practices, whether the NGSS explicitly "asks" you to or not.

Similarly, science content very often has blurry borders. The entire modern electric energy grid is a massive energy transfer machine, where coal or gas is burned in a central location and the resulting energy is transferred to our homes in the form of electricity. This electricity can then be converted back into heat or light or useful work. For example, the DCI *PS3.B: Conservation of Energy and Energy Transfer* specifically mentions this transfer of energy through electric circuits (NGSS Lead States, 2013c). The following NGSS performance expectation specifically mentions electric current:

4-PS3–2. *Make observations* to provide evidence that energy can be transferred from place to place by sound, light, heat, and electric currents.

LS1.D: Information Processing is a life sciences DCI that specifically addresses electrical signals that propagate through the nervous system, where "each sense receptor responds to different inputs, transmitting them as signals that travel along nerve cells to the brain" (NGSS Lead States, 2013a, p. 4). Although the focus of *PS3.D Energy in chemical processes and everyday life* as listed in the NGSS progression guide appears to be on photosynthesis, modern energy storage systems we all encounter in our day-to-day lives are based on chemical batteries. In fact, at a fundamental level, most of the critical processes governing cell behavior in our bodies rely on electric potential differences (voltages!). We literally can't get away from topics in electric circuits.

It may seem like I'm trying to make an argument for including circuits as a topic for your teaching. I am. But the bigger point I'm trying to make here is that you (and the leaders in your school district) need to be careful when reading the NGSS and designing curriculum that is consistent with the standards. Just because a topic isn't explicitly listed in the NGSS, doesn't mean that it is not to be taught. The NGSS says students should be taught energy transfer. How do we do that? One good way could be through circuits. However, maybe some other domain will work best for your population. Realize that the NGSS *does* give you flexibility to make these decisions, as long as you're mindful about teaching content *through* the practice of science. I hope the leaders in your school district similarly value this flexibility.

Summary

This book both started and ended with Figure 7.8 outlining the science practices and how they are connected. The focus in your classroom needs to be on this process and these practices if you wish to create new scientists. We've looked at individual examples of how to weave together practice and content in the classroom. In this chapter, we discussed how to put it all together in capstone experiences. In particular, we looked at what a capstone is and what a capstone is good for accomplishing. I went through an example capstone experience on circuits. Finally, we discussed the importance of going beyond the NGSS with respect to both content and which practices to use for that content.

The following is a brief summary of the main points:

- Capstones are explorations that students complete with little guidance and that tie together the science practices across the dimensions of investigation, interpretation, and communication.
- Capstones come at the end of learning units, because content knowledge is typically necessary for authentic exploration.
- A good capstone lesson accomplishes the following:
    - it reinforces previously learned material,
    - has students use practices in new ways, and
    - promotes expert-like views about science.
- The NGSS is a set of minimum standards and not curriculum.
- You can go beyond the NGSS with respect to content.
- You can and should go beyond the explicit performance expectations in the NGSS. Science practices do not have well-defined borders.
- Focus on science as a process, and you will create new scientists.

References

American Association of Physics Teachers. (2013, February 1). *Summary of the AAPT Response to the January 2013 Draft Next Generation Science Standards*. Retrieved from AAPT.ORG: www.aapt.org/Resources/policy/upload/AAPT_Summary_of_NGSS_Response_1_February_2013.pdf

Hestenes, I., & Halloun, D. (1998). Interpreting VASS dimensions and profiles. *Science & Education, 7*(6), 553–577.

Moore, J. C., & Rubbo, L. J. (2016). Modeling hidden circuits: An authentic research experience in one lab period. *The Physics Teacher, 54*(7), 423.

National Research Council. (2012). *A Framework for K–12 Science Education: Practices, Crosscutting Concepts, and Core Ideas.* Washington, DC: The National Academies Press.

NGSS Lead States. (2013a). APPENDIX E—Progressions Within the Next Generation Science Standards. In N. L. States (Ed.), *Next Generation Science Standards: For States, by States.* Washington, DC: The National Academies Press.

NGSS Lead States. (2013b). *Next Generation Science Standards: For States, by States.* Washington, DC: The National Academies Press.

NGSS Lead States. (2013c). Standards by DCI. In N. L. States (Ed.), *The Next Generation Science Standards: For States, by States.* Washington, DC: The National Academies Press.

Polya, G. (2004). *How to Solve It: A New Aspect of Mathematical Method.* Princeton, NJ: Princeton University Press.

South Carolina Department of Education. (2014). *South Carolina Academic Standards and Performance Indicators for Science.* Columbia, SC: State Board of Education.

For Product Safety Concerns and Information please contact our EU representative GPSR@taylorandfrancis.com
Taylor & Francis Verlag GmbH, Kaufingerstraße 24, 80331 München, Germany

www.ingramcontent.com/pod-product-compliance
Lightning Source LLC
Chambersburg PA
CBHW080937300426
44115CB00017B/2856